The Loveday Method®

The Bridge of Possibility

The Library, The Crystal
and
The Coat of a Thousand Lives

Three Books

The Origin of
The Loveday Method®

A Trilogy

By

Geoffrey Loveday

The Origin of The Loveday Method

The Library, The Crystal and The Coat of a Thousand Lives; Threads of the Forgotten

Author: Geoffrey Loveday

Copyright © 2025 by Geoffrey Loveday - All Rights Reserved.

The right of Geoffrey Loveday to be identified as author of this work has been asserted by the author in accordance with section 77 and 78 of the Copyright, Designs and Patents Act 1988.

First Published in 2025
ISBN 978-1-917978-12-5 (Paperback)
978-1-917978-13-2 (Hardback)
978-1-917978-14-9 (E-Book)

Book cover designed and layout by: Geoffrey Loveday

Published by:

Mindlayers Publishing
35-37 Ludgate Hill,
London England,
EC4M 7JN

Website: www.liverpoolhypnosis.co.uk

Authors and publishers cannot be held responsible for any consequences that result from the usage of information in this book.

The author or the publisher assumes no responsibility or liability for how you use the information contained herein.

A CIP catalogue record for this title is available from the British Library.

All rights reserved. No part of this book may be reproduced or translated by any form or by any means, electronic or mechanical, including photocopying, recording or by any information storage and retrieval system without written permission from the author.

The novel is entirely a work of fiction. The names, characters, and incidents portrayed in it are the work of the author's imagination. Any resemblance to actual persons, living or dead, events or localities is entirely incidental. The views expressed by the fictional characters do not necessarily reflect the views of the author.

I wonder where life will take us now ...

And so the journey begins.

Let me take you on this magical adventure.

Contents

About the Author 10
Dedication 12
Inspiration 15
The Akashic Library of Life 18
    The Man from 1893 18
    The First Scribes - The Origin of the Akashic Library ... 23
    The Sinking of the Lusitania — Jonathan's Journey through the Doorway of Time 32
    The Lost Manuscript of the Akashic Library 41
    Chapter One: The Red Chair 48
    Chapter Two: The Life of Aelius 55
    Chapter Three: The Mask and the Key 60
    Chapter Four: The Hunters in the Stacks 65
    Chapter Five: The Tower Without Doors 71
    Chapter Six: The Stairs That Weren't There 75
    Chapter Seven: The Man in the Alley 79
    Chapter Eight: The Wing of Echoes 84
    Chapter Nine: The Crimson Truth 88
    Chapter Ten: The Prophecy of Fire 93
    Chapter Eleven: The Blank Book 98
    Chapter Twelve: The Last Seizure 102
    Chapter Thirteen — The Doorway of Return ... 108
    Chapter Fourteen: Seeds of Return 111
    Chapter Fifteen: The Unseen Awakening 114
    Chapter Sixteen: The First Circle 117
    Chapter Seventeen: The Veil Unmasked 121

Chapter Eighteen: Preparing the Circle 125

Chapter Nineteen: The First Strike 128

Chapter Twenty: The Awakening Tide 133

Chapter Twenty-One: The Coat of a Thousand Lives .. 138

The Crystal: A Touch Through Time 143

  The Book of Echoes 143

  The Crystal 146

    The Crystal of Echoes 147

    Aira the Silent 150

    The Warrior Who Could Not Win, and the Book That Remembered 154

    Ivenna the Watcher 158

  Chapter One: The Crystal and the Echo 162

  Chapter Two: The Broken Voice 168

  Chapter Three: The Bride of Silence 175

    The Wanderer Who Forgot, and the Memory That Found Them 181

    The Monarch Who Chose Her Soul Over Her Throne 185

The Coat of a Thousand Lives 189

  Why I write this 189

  "The Soul Remembers", by Geoffrey Loveday 191

  What are the Threads of the Forgotten? 195

  How "The Loveday Method" Brought One Man Back from the Edge of Life 200

The Beginning: The Return of the Hidden Ones 208

Chapter One: The Scribe's Silence 211

Chapter Two: The Midwife's Fire 216

Chapter Three: The Last Flight 223

Chapter Four: The Warning 228

Chapter Five: The Temple of the Silent Star 234

Chapter Six: Sarah - The First Thread 239

Chapter Seven: The Coat that didn't Belong 246

Chapter Eight: The Fear That Wore a Mask 257

Chapter Nine: Alan - The Forgotten Orders 263

   Anna – The Archivist's Thread (Present Day) 269

   Anna – The First Life (Unknown Era) 271

Chapter Ten: The Keeper 274

Chapter Eleven: Threads Yet to Be Told 278

Chapter Twelve: The Ink That Never Dried 280

Chapter Thirteen: The Life That Hasn't Happened Yet 286

Chapter Fourteen: David – The Thousand Lives 291

Chapter Fifteen: The Girl of Tongues 296

Chapter Sixteen: The Coal Dust Dreamer 298

Chapter Seventeen: The Weight of Stone 304

Chapter Eighteen: The Silence Beneath the Floorboards
.... 307

Chapter Nineteen: The Bones of the Earth 311

Chapter Twenty: The Enchanted Mirror – A Life Remembered 317

Chapter Twenty One: The Boy Who Carried a Century of Fear 321

Chapter Twenty Two: The One Who Knew His Name . 327

Chapter Twenty Three: The Keeper's Return 331

Chapter Twenty Four: The First Silence 335

Chapter Twenty Five: The Echo in Your Hands............ 340
Final Reflection 344
Dedication 347
About the Author 348
Coming In 2025 350

About the Author

My name is Geoffrey Loveday. Like you, I'm on a journey—one shaped by experience, reflection, and a deep desire to find meaning in both the beauty and the ache of being human.

I've written twelve books. I hold credentials, professional titles, and years of experience. But none of that truly explains why I do this work. The real reason? There's a quiet voice inside me—persistent, ancient, and alive—that calls me to write. Not to impress, but to connect. To tell the truth. To offer something real.

I don't write because I have the answers. I write because I believe truth—honest, raw, human truth—is sacred. I believe healing begins with honesty. And I believe that when we tell our stories from the heart, we remember we're not alone.

My work isn't about fixing anyone. It's about guiding people back to what's already within them—the parts untouched by noise, wounds, or expectations. Underneath all of that, there is wholeness. There is you.

Through The Loveday Method and Inherited Therapy, I don't come as a healer or a guru, but as someone who's been there—who continues to begin again. As a certified hypnoanalyst, clinical hypnotherapy instructor, and witness to thousands of personal transformations, I've seen what's possible when we simply remember who we are.

Lasting change doesn't come from force—it comes from remembering. From returning. From reconnecting with the truth we carry in our bones.

I don't consider myself special. But I do know this calling is real. And I offer what I've learned with the hope that it finds its way to the hearts that need it most.

This is my work. This is my offering.

Dedication

This book is a tribute—an offering—to the extraordinary souls who have shaped my life with quiet strength, deep wisdom, and boundless love. You are not only in my memories—you are in my breath, my choices, and my voice. You are in these pages.

To my father—your calm, steady presence lives on in me. Though your voice is now silence, I hear you in moments of stillness, feel your hand in the steadying of my own. You taught me the strength of quiet love—the kind that endures, anchors, and guides, long after the words are gone.

To my mother—our time together was brief, but your light was fierce and lasting. You taught me to hold beauty in fragile hands, to cherish what truly matters. Your tenderness still moves through my life like a soft current, ever-present, ever-giving.

To my grandparents, aunts, and uncles—your stories, your love, your grace built the foundation upon which I stand. You gave me roots, a sense of home I carry with me always.

To Alma and Leon—your open arms welcomed me without hesitation. Your quiet generosity and warmth have left marks on my life that words can only begin to express. Thank you for making love feel so expansive.

To my beloved wife—though you walk beyond this world, you remain closer than ever. I feel you in the small, sacred spaces—in our children's laughter, in the hush of dawn, in the strength I didn't know I had. Your belief in me continues to be the compass by which I navigate. You are in every word, every breath, and every line of this book.

To our children—you are my why. My strength. My greatest teachers. You've shown me how love bends, stretches, and grows even through pain. In you, I see hop, and I am endlessly grateful.

To my grandchildren—your wonder brings light into every shadow. Your joy reminds me that life renews itself, that love carries forward, and that the future holds beauty still unfolding.

To my sons-in-law—thank you for choosing to stand beside us—not just in name, but in heart. Your presence enriches our family in ways that matter deeply.

To my brothers—I carry your absence with reverence. The ache of missing you is matched only by the strength your memory brings. Your laughter, your pride—they echo in me. You remain part of every forward step I take.

To my friends, mentors, and fellow travellers—your belief in me was never unnoticed. In both the quiet and the storm, your presence made the difference. Thank you for holding space, for reminding me who I am when I forgot.

This book is yours as much as it is mine. Your love is its rhythm. Your influence, its spine. Every word is laced with the gratitude I feel for having walked alongside you. Thank you—for your love, your light, and your legacy.

Always.

Inspiration

This book was born from the quiet heroism I've witnessed in hospital corridors, waiting rooms, bedside whispers, and long nights filled with uncertainty.

It is a tribute to those walking through illness with courage, grace, and a strength that defies explanation. If you are fighting, recovering, or simply finding your way—you are the soul of these pages.

To those who have shared their journeys so openly: you've given more than your stories. You've given us insight into the depth of human resilience.

You've shown that bravery doesn't always look loud—it often appears in soft footsteps, trembling hands, and the decision to carry on, even when you don't know how.

To the doctors, nurses, researchers, and medical professionals: your commitment does more than treat illness. It restores dignity, provides hope, and often gives people back their lives.

Your work reaches far beyond charts and procedures—it touches hearts, and it changes futures.

To the carers, families, and loved ones who show up, again and again—you are the quiet force that keeps others going.

Your patience, loyalty, and unspoken acts of love form a kind of strength no title can capture.

To the organisations and charities that advocate, educate, and offer support—you are the lifeline many never see coming but come to rely on.

Your passion creates real, lasting change, the kind that can never be measured by statistics alone.

To my readers—thank you for picking up this book with an open mind and a compassionate heart. By engaging with these stories, you help create a space for empathy, for connection, and for healing.

You are part of the change.

And to those behind the scenes—mentors, editors, loved ones—thank you. Your belief in this project carried it from an idea into something that can now reach others.

Your support has meant everything.

This is more than a book. It's a celebration of human spirit—of the will to keep going, to keep loving, and to keep hoping, even when the road ahead is unclear.

Thank you for being part of it.

The Akashic Library of Life

The Man from 1893

When he first walked into my office, his face carried the tightness of a man worn thin—not just by addiction, but by shame, by secrets too old to name. He wasn't a gambler in the way people usually think. He wasn't chasing money.

He was chasing a silence—trying to quiet something ancient and hungry inside him.

"I don't know why I do it," he told me. "It's like... I black out. I'm not even there."

He was ready to go deeper.

So that day, I guided him into a trance, deeper than before. Deeper than memory. Deeper than this life.

And when I spoke the words that opened the way, I saw his breath change. Something inside him stirred. Something old.

I led him to the *Akashic Library of Life*—not a place you can find on any map, but one that lives in the space between thought and soul. It is a sacred archive, holding the story of every soul's journey—every past life, every ancestor's choice, every forgotten crossroads. It is the divine web that connects everything, the blueprint of consciousness itself.

In his mind's eye, he began climbing a staircase that rose out of a velvet fog. Step by step, he ascended into the unknown, until he reached a great oak door, ancient and humming with energy. He pushed it open and entered the Library.

It took his breath away.

Vaulted ceilings disappeared into the stars. Shelves towered like cathedrals, lined with glowing scrolls, crystal-bound tomes, and memories suspended in liquid light. The air vibrated with wisdom, with soul.

He wandered, drawn not by logic, but by instinct—his soul knew the way. Deep in the heart of the Library, he found a single chair. Plain. Wooden. Waiting.

The moment he sat down, time cracked.

The world around him dissolved, and he was no longer the man sitting in my office. He was someone else entirely.

He awoke in the body of a 40-year-old man. The year was 1893. A gray city pressed in on all sides—smoke, soot, the clang of machinery, and the cries of the desperate. He wore a threadbare coat and callused hands. His pockets were empty, and his soul was heavy.

He was running out of options. A moneylender waited for him in the shadows of a narrow alley. He should never have gone. But desperation is a cruel god. And back then, he bowed to it.

Under hypnosis, his voice thickened. It aged. "I didn't do it just once," he whispered. "I kept going back... until I had nothing left."

Then, his voice broke.

"There was a child. A boy. He died. I couldn't save him."

The loss was too much. In that life, it hollowed him out. He blamed himself. The grief became a noose he could never untie. He lost his family. His dignity. Himself.

And now, lifetimes later, the same compulsion was returning in a new disguise—gambling, this time—but it wasn't about the cards. It was about trying to rewrite a failure that never stopped bleeding.

The journey through the Akashic Library had not been random. It was a reckoning. A soul reaching across time, across death, to say: *Not again.*

The past life had become a bridge—a mirror held up to the present. The lesson was clear, urgent, and haunting:

Some losses are not punishments. They are turning points. And if you carry guilt across lifetimes, it will bury you.

In the stillness of the trance, I spoke softly: "You are not that man anymore. But he needs you. Forgive him."

And in the silence that followed, something shifted.

A release.

A thread untangled.

When he opened his eyes, tears streamed down his face, but his hands were steady. The room felt different—like something ancient had finally exhaled.

He had glimpsed the truth: we are more than our habits. We are echoes of who we've been, and architects of who we choose to become.

And the Akashic Library never forgets.

The First Scribes - The Origin of the Akashic Library

Long before the first sunrise, before the rivers carved their beds or the mountains lifted their crowns, there was only the Stillness. In that Stillness moved the **First Scribes** — beings older than time, born from the breath of the Infinite.

They were not gods. They were not mortal. They were the Witnesses.

And their task was sacred: to record every thought, every choice, every heartbeat that had ever been — and ever would be — into a single, eternal record. From their hands came the **Akashic Library**, a hall so vast that its shelves curved beyond sight, its books bound in light itself.

But the Library was not merely a place of memory. It was a map. A design. For the Scribes had seen the future of humanity — the glories and the ruins, the triumphs and the sorrows — and they knew the path ahead would be treacherous.

They understood that for humanity to survive, we would need to remember more than our own small lifetimes.

We would need to remember *all* of them.

The first to walk its halls was not a Scribe but a soul — a soul who had agreed, before birth, to carry the stories of many lives. His name is lost now, but his choice is remembered.

In the Stillness-before-Time, he stepped before the Scribes and said:

"I wish to live, not once, but many times. I wish to taste every joy, suffer every sorrow, and carry the memory so that others may learn without falling where I have fallen."

And so the Scribes gave him his first book — empty, but waiting.

Each life he lived filled its pages, and each return to the Library was a chance to choose again — to rewrite, to repair, to continue the story

The old legends whisper that before each birth, every soul stands before the Library. We walk its shelves, tracing our fingers over the spines of books we have written in other lives. We pause at a particular volume — perhaps one not yet complete — and we open it.

Inside are the beginnings of the life to come. The place we will be born. The lessons we have yet to learn. The bonds we must make — or break — to finish the story.

And we choose.

Not all is fixed. The ending is unwritten, the paths many. But the challenges, the turning points, the seeds of joy and sorrow — these we select ourselves.

For the Library is not a prison of fate. It is the workshop of the soul.

The First Scribes never left us. They still walk the unseen corridors, their hands moving over the books, adding what we cannot remember. They whisper into dreams, nudge us toward certain choices, and sometimes, when the weight of the story becomes too much, they guide a seeker back to the Library while still alive — so they may look upon their own book and understand.

It is said that when a soul finishes its last volume, when every lesson is learned and every wound is healed, the Scribes close the book and place it on a high shelf where no shadow reaches. That soul needs no more lifetimes — it has become part of the Library itself, helping others find their way.

The Scribes foresaw that humanity would one day forget where its suffering began. The pain of generations would echo down through the centuries, wearing new faces but carrying the same weight.

And so, they created a way back. They designed the Library not only for the dead but for the living — for those who could be guided to it while still in their current lifetime, so they might open the book and see the truth for themselves.

The path is hidden, yet it has been rediscovered by those who know how to lead another soul inward. One such path is known today as **The Loveday Method**.

And so, dear reader, the question remains: When you were still in the Stillness-before-Time, when the shelves of the Akashic Library stretched endlessly before you, when the Scribes asked which book you would open next...

What did you choose?

They told you the Akashic Library was only a legend. They lied.

It has been here since before the first spark of creation — a vault beyond the reach of time where every soul is written. Some call it *The Book of the Unknown*. Others, *The Book of Echoes*. The oldest tongues had no name for it at all, only silence, and to speak of it was to disturb the stillness in which all truth rests.

The **Akashic Library of Life** — whispered of in prophecy, feared in legend, and revered in silence — is a place beyond the measure of time, a vault where the stories of every soul are etched in light. It is said to have existed before the first dawn, before the birth of stars, before even the thought of creation stirred. In the ancient scriptures, its names are many: *The Book of the Unknown, The Book of Echoes*, and others lost to the crumbling tongues of ages long forgotten.

Within its boundless halls, entire worlds hang suspended in stillness. The air hums with the weight of a billion lifetimes — their memories, their choices, their triumphs, their ruin. Here, the truth of all that has been is kept, not as a sentence of fate, but as a mirror for those who dare to see.

The ancients spoke of a **rite of passage**, a journey taken only by those willing to face what most spend their lives avoiding. It begins with a single step onto the **Great Staircase**.

Each stone, worn smooth by seekers across eons, rises into a mist that swallows the horizon. With every step upward, the weight of the present loosens; the heartbeat falls in rhythm with something older, something infinite.

At last, the summit. A single door stands there — plain, silent, waiting. It does not open to touch alone; it opens to readiness. And when it swings wide, the seeker steps into the Akashic Library itself — a realm where past, present, and future do not follow one another, but exist together, woven into the same endless breath.

The corridors stretch beyond sight, lined with shelves that seem carved from light and shadow both. Whispers rise from the walls — voices calling from lifetimes past, some your own, some not. And somewhere deep within, a chair waits. Not grand. Not gilded. Yet the air around it thrums like the heartbeat of the universe.

When the seeker sits, the Library shifts. The air folds. The self unravels. Time becomes water, and you are carried into another life — one you have never lived, yet whose weight you have carried all along. You walk its streets, feel its griefs, taste its moments of despair, until the truth reveals itself: this burden was never yours.

And then comes the surrender — the giving back. Like a stone dropped into the depths, the weight falls away. The breath deepens. Light rushes in. Chains uncoil from the heart. The soul rises — lighter than air, clearer than dawn, unbound from the invisible sorrow it has carried for lifetimes.

The Library watches in silence. Another page is turned. Another story set free. And somewhere, deep within its endless halls, your true self takes its first unshackled step toward becoming.

The Sinking of the Lusitania — Jonathan's Journey through the Doorway of Time

It began, as these journeys often do, in stillness.

Jonathan lay back in the chair, his breathing soft and slow, and his eyes closed but moving faintly beneath the lids. I guided him deeper — past the hum of the present moment, past the noise of thought, into the quiet waters of the subconscious.

He was sixty-six years young, with a loving wife, two children, and a granddaughter who lit up his world. And yet, a shadow lingered over his life: a fear of leaving home. Holidays that should have brought joy ended early in panic. Trips were cut short. His chest would tighten, his pulse race, his mind scream that he had to return — now.

**THE SINKING OF THE LUSITANIA –
JONATHAN'S JOURNEY THROUGH THE DORWAY OF TIME**

When I asked him what he wanted most, his wish was heartbreakingly simple: *"I just want to enjoy my holiday."*

I told Jonathan we would seek the answer in the **Akashic Library** — the eternal archive of every soul's journey.

The moment I spoke the word *library*, his breathing deepened. "I see... shelves," he murmured. "Endless shelves. And... a chair."

He described it slowly, as if the act of seeing was also the act of remembering: old red leather, worn smooth, cracked in places from decades — maybe centuries — of use. The air around it felt heavy, expectant.

"Sit," I instructed. "And when you do, you will travel back to the moment where this fear began — even if it was generations before you were born."

Jonathan lowered himself into the chair. The library shifted. The walls folded inward, the light bent, and the air thickened until there was nothing but silence — and then, another world.

"Sit," I instructed. "And when you do, you will travel back to the moment where this fear began — even if it was generations before you were born."

Jonathan lowered himself into the chair. The library shifted. The walls folded inward, the light bent, and the air thickened until there was nothing but silence — and then, another world.

"It's 1915," Jonathan said, his voice softer now, distant. "I'm... I'm not me."

He described looking down at himself — broad hands, rough from labour, a sailor's uniform snug against his frame. His heart was heavy, swollen with the ache of homesickness.

"I miss them... my family," he whispered. "It's been so long... I can't stand it anymore."

"What's the date?" I asked.

"May 1st, 1915. Pier 54. New York. I'm boarding the Lusitania."

He paused, and I felt the moment settle around us. The RMS *Lusitania* — one of the grandest ocean liners of her age — towered before him, her funnels rising like golden chimneys against the morning light.

Passengers bustled about, luggage clattered against the dock, and seagulls wheeled overhead. He was going home to Liverpool.

He did not yet know this would be his final voyage.

The scene blurred, then sharpened. "It's May 7th," Jonathan said. "We're close to Ireland... I can almost smell the sea there."

His tone shifted. Urgency crept in. "I'm a stoker... down in the furnace room. The heat is... suffocating. It's so loud — the roar of the boilers — I can feel it in my teeth."

Then, a sudden jolt. The sound of metal shrieking. A boom that swallowed the air.

"It's... the water," he gasped. "It's everywhere — pouring in so fast. I can't..." His voice broke. "I'll never see them again. My family... I can't..."

The panic in his voice was raw. He was no longer describing — he was *reliving*. The cold rushed in. The ship groaned as if alive, dying. Men shouted, the sound drowned in the roar of the sea filling every space. In that moment, Jonathan was his great-great-grandfather, trapped in the belly of a doomed ship, knowing the end had come.

"Jonathan," I said firmly, pulling him just far enough back to remember himself. "You are not him. He is not you. Tell him what I say."

Through him, I spoke the words of release:

"I will honour your memories, but I cannot and will not carry your misery any longer. All the agony, suffering, and unhappy feelings you had in life are not mine. It is unfair that I should bear the weight of your shame, your longing, and your inability to leave home. They are yours. I give them back."

Jonathan's body shuddered. His breath came faster. He whispered, "Something's leaving me."

I could feel it too — a dark, heavy presence lifting away from him, flowing back into the spirit of the man he had once been.

And then, the transformation: the darkness dissolved, and a **golden light** spilled down as if the heavens had opened. It wrapped around them both — warm, unending, absolute.

Jonathan looked into his great-great-grandfather's eyes. He saw love. Relief. Peace.

His ancestor smiled, turned toward a brilliant doorway, and stepped forward. Just before passing through, he looked back — and in that final glance was gratitude, freedom, and farewell.

And then he was gone.

Jonathan and his great-great-grandfather had been trapped together in a moment of history — one in death, one in life — bound by the same longing to return home. In that chair, in that library beyond time, both were freed.

When Jonathan emerged from the trance, there was a stillness in him where before there had been tension. His chest no longer carried the invisible weight.

For the first time in his life, he could imagine leaving home without fear. Because now, he understood: the longing that had haunted him was never his. It belonged to a man lost in 1915, 11 nautical miles from the Irish coast, who never made it home.

And on this day, more than a century later, they both finally did.

The Lost Manuscript of the Akashic Library

For centuries, it was only a rumour — a book no scholar could prove existed, spoken of in fragments, whispers, and footnotes buried in older works. The *Manuscript of the First Library*.

It was said to contain not only the origin of the Akashic Library but instructions — precise, unflinching instructions — on how to reach it while still alive.

In the year 1495, deep in the candlelit quiet of his Milan workshop, **Leonardo da Vinci** stumbled upon it. The parchment was brittle, the ink faded, but the drawings and script within were unlike anything he had seen before. Not only did it speak of the **Akashic Library** — the eternal archive of every soul's journey — it contained a name he would never forget:

"Il Metodo Loveday." (*The Loveday Method.*)

In the year 1495, deep in the candlelit quiet of his Milan workshop, Leonardo da Vinci stumbled upon it. The parchment was brittle, the ink faded, but the drawings and script within were unlike he had seen before.

Not only did it speak of the Akashic Library — the eternal archive of every soul's journey — it contained a name he would never forget:

IL METOD LOVEDAY
(THE LOVEDAY METHOD.)

The drawings were impossibly precise — spiral staircases disappearing into light, strange celestial diagrams, and human figures seated in ornate chairs, their forms surrounded by radiant halos. Between the illustrations ran a text in an older Italian hand, its letters fading but legible.

It spoke of a place beyond time — *La Biblioteca Akashica*, the Akashic Library — where the story of every soul was written. "Through the Path of Stillness," the manuscript said, "one may open the Book of their own Soul, witness the lives they have lived, and alter the course of those yet to come."

Leonardo read on, his eyes widening. The text spoke of a connection between memory, lineage, and choice — of how the griefs and fears of ancestors could be inherited like blood and bone, and how, by returning them to their origin, a soul could be freed.

It ended with a warning:

"When the world thirsts for power, keep the Method hidden. When the heart of mankind longs for truth above conquest, the Method shall return."

Leonardo leaned back, the candlelight catching the reflection in his eyes. He knew instantly: the world was not ready.

By morning, the manuscript was hidden — sewn into the false lining of a cedar chest, its pages surrounded by sketches of machines and anatomical studies, disguised among his more ordinary works. Only he would know its true value.

It had been catalogued as *Codice V.318*, part of an auction lot of Renaissance papers. Most of the bidders wanted the diagrams of bridges and flying machines. Only one man noticed the faint glint of gold leaf in the title hidden inside.

Dr. Adrian Cole — historian, linguist, and reluctant believer in the supernatural — held the manuscript under the museum light.

The words curved across the page in mirrored script, Leonardo's unmistakable hand:

"Il Metodo Loveday." (*The Loveday Method*)

Adrian frowned. He had heard the term once before — buried in an obscure 19th-century treatise on mystical traditions — but never linked to Leonardo. The translation began easily enough, but as he worked deeper into the text, something strange began to happen.

He dreamed.

Not ordinary dreams — but vivid scenes from other lives. A soldier in a smoky forest, barefoot in the cold earth. A sailor stoking the furnaces of a great ship. A woman in a candlelit room, her hands trembling over a sealed letter.

The manuscript was doing something to him.

Each night he translated, the dreams grew stronger. And with them, a strange pull — a sense that the Library Leonardo had written of was real, and that *Il Metodo Loveday* was not merely an idea, but an invitation.

The text guided him step by step: how to still the mind, how to reach the "Red Chair of Returning," how to move between lifetimes as if turning pages in a book.

Adrian began to wonder — had Leonardo himself walked those halls? Was that why he hid it, fearing what might happen if the power fell into the wrong hands?

On the final night of translation, Adrian sat in his study, the manuscript open before him. The last page read:

"When the reader has come to this line, they are no longer reading — they are remembering. Close your eyes, sit, and return."

He did.

The room fell away. Shelves rose around him, higher than mountains, glowing faintly in the dim air. Somewhere in the distance, he saw it — an old red leather chair, its surface cracked with age, waiting.

And Adrian Cole understood. Leonardo had been right. The world had not been ready.

Until now.

Chapter One: The Red Chair

The candle on Adrian Cole's desk burned low, its wax pooling over the edge in slow drips. The last page of *Il Metodo Loveday* lay open before him, Leonardo's mirrored script glinting faintly in the dim light.

He had translated it all — the breathing sequences, the mental focus exercises, the precise posture required to "shift the soul through the corridors of time." But it was the final instruction that unsettled him most:

"When you have read this far, you are no longer reading — you are remembering. Close your eyes, sit, and return."

He leaned back in his chair, half-smiling at the audacity of it. *Remembering*, as though he had been there before. As though these instructions were not something to learn, but something to recall.

And yet... the manuscript had already changed him. The dreams. The uncanny clarity in his thoughts. The feeling that his life had been moving toward this exact moment all along.

He closed his eyes.

The world tilted. The hum of the city outside vanished. When he opened his eyes again, his study was gone.

Shelves — impossibly tall, curving away into shadow — rose all around him. Each one was lined with books whose covers shimmered faintly, some golden, some silver, some the deep black of midnight. The air was heavy with a quiet that seemed alive.

And there, ahead of him, stood the **Red Leather Chair**.

It looked exactly as Leonardo had sketched it — worn smooth by centuries of use, the cracks in its surface like veins of time itself.

He sat.

The instant he touched the chair, the Library shifted. The shelves spun without moving. The air bent, folded, and drew him through itself as if it were a page turning in a book.

When the world steadied, he was standing in a small candlelit chamber. The air smelled of parchment and beeswax. Across from him sat a man in a long robe, his face shadowed by a hood. On the table between them lay three books:

The Book of the Unknown. The Book of Echoes. And a third, its title in a language Adrian couldn't read.

The man spoke without looking up. "You've come far too soon."

Adrian's heart hammered. "Who are you?"

The man lifted his head, and Adrian caught his breath. The eyes staring back at him were his own.

"I am the first Scribe," the man said softly. "The one who began the Library. These books," he rested his hands on them, "are not just records. They are keys. *The Book of the Unknown* reveals what was never lived but might have been. *The Book of Echoes* shows the patterns that repeat across your lifetimes. And the third—" He tapped the cover. "—is not for you. Not yet."

"These books have been hidden in the folds of history. Scattered through the ages, protected by those who would forget their own purpose. They await the seekers who dare to remember.

"You must find them — not to claim them, but to unite them. Only then will the world be free."

The Scribe reached into a drawer and withdrew a pair of spectacles unlike any Adrian had seen — the lenses clear as crystal, the frames etched with tiny constellations.

"These will let you see the Library as it truly is," the Scribe said. "Not just the shelves, but the lives within."

Adrian hesitated, then took them. The moment he put them on, the room dissolved again — and he was walking through corridors where books opened themselves as he passed, spilling scenes into the air like smoke:

A woman weeping over a sealed letter. A boy running through a field beneath a sky split by lightning. A soldier in the forest, sword in hand, barefoot in the mud.

He stopped. That last one — the soldier — turned, and Adrian felt the shock of recognition. This was no stranger. This was himself... in another life.

The Scribe's voice echoed in his ears, though the man was nowhere in sight.

"These books are bound to you. The Loveday Method is the doorway, but the spectacles show the truth. The Book of the Unknown will tempt you. The Book of Echoes will haunt you. And somewhere in this Library, there is a fourth book — yours — still unfinished. When you find it, your life will change in ways you cannot yet imagine."

The world began to fold again, drawing him upward through the shelves toward another page, another scene.

When Adrian's vision cleared, he was no longer in the Library.

He was standing in the middle of a Roman marketplace in 10 AD. And he knew — without being told — that the man beside him, haggling for grain, was the one who had written The Book of the Unknown.

The journey had only just begun.

Chapter Two: The Life of Aelius

The air in the marketplace was alive with noise — traders shouting their wares, the clatter of pottery, the bleating of goats tied to wooden posts. The sun was high, warm on Adrian's skin. But it wasn't his skin.

He looked down at his arms — thicker, bronzed by years of work. A coarse tunic hung loose over his frame. Around his neck, a small bronze pendant glinted in the light.

He heard a voice behind him. "Aelius! Come — the grain seller is trying to cheat me again."

Adrian turned and saw him: a man in his thirties, sharp-eyed, with the easy authority of someone used to being obeyed. This was the man who would write *The Book of the Unknown*.

Aelius followed, or perhaps Adrian did — it was hard to tell now where one ended and the other began. The marketplace shifted subtly as they moved, stalls rearranging themselves as though the scene was alive, aware of his presence.

As they stopped at the grain seller's stall, Aelius spoke quietly, almost as if to himself. "There are patterns in the world, Adrian. Paths people walk without knowing. You can see them if you look long enough."

Adrian froze. "How do you know my name?"

Aelius smiled faintly. "Because I've seen you before."

From beneath his tunic, Aelius produced a small leather-bound volume — worn, stained, but sturdy. The title was pressed into the cover in faint gold:

The Book of Echoes.

He opened it, and the pages came alive. Scenes rose from the parchment — not drawings, not words, but memories, glowing like firelight in the air.

A woman kneeling beside a fallen soldier. A child on a ship, staring at the endless sea. A man, stoking a furnace deep in the belly of a great vessel.

Adrian recognised them all.

"These are your lives," Aelius said simply. "Not just this one, not just the one you remember — all of them. Every choice, every loss, every longing that has shaped you."

Adrian reached out to touch the page, and the marketplace dissolved. The two men stood now in a long, dim corridor of the Akashic Library. The walls pulsed with faint light, as if alive.

Aelius closed the book. "*The Book of the Unknown* tells you what might have been, the paths untaken. *The Book of Echoes* shows you the patterns you keep repeating. But neither can change your path. For that, you need the fourth book — your own — and the key to unlock it."

Adrian felt the weight of the spectacles in his pocket.

"The Loveday Method?" he asked.

Aelius nodded. "The Method is the bridge. It is how you walk between lives while still alive. It is how you return what is not yours to carry."

Aelius stepped closer, lowering his voice. "But there is a danger. The Book of the Unknown will call to you. It will offer you visions of lives where you were richer, braver, and more powerful. It will tell you that you could still have them. If you follow it, you will lose yourself."

Adrian thought of Leonardo's warning. For centuries the manuscript had been hidden.

"What am I supposed to do?"

Aelius handed him *The Book of Echoes*. "You start here. See the patterns. Break them. Only then can you finish your own story."

The corridor blurred, and Adrian felt the strange, weightless pull again — the Library turning another page. Aelius' voice echoed as the scene faded:

"Remember this; the Echoes are not chains. They are invitations to choose differently."

The shelves stretched away into light. The red leather chair waited for him once more. And Adrian knew the next time he sat, another life — another echo — would open.

And somewhere in those pages, the truth about the creator of *The Book of the Unknown*... and the fate of all the enchanted books... was waiting.

Chapter Three: The Mask and the Key

The red leather chair creaked under Adrian's weight as he sat again. The air in the Library shifted instantly — a low vibration through the floor, the smell of something faintly metallic, the sense that the shelves themselves were leaning closer.

He closed his eyes.

When he opened them, the world was awash in gold and shadow. Lanterns glowed in the fog. Gondolas drifted along dark canals. Above the water, balconies draped with silk banners leaned toward each other like gossiping neighbours.

Venice. The year — he somehow knew — was 1623.

He was standing in a crowded square lit by torches. Men in long cloaks and women in masks moved through the crowd, their laughter mingling with the music of a distant lute. The air was heavy with perfume and the salt of the lagoon.

A figure in a black half-mask approached, gloved hands clasped before them. The voice — low, precise — cut through the noise.

"You have the spectacles?"

Adrian reached into his coat — though it wasn't his modern coat but a fine wool doublet — and felt the cool metal frames in his palm. He nodded.

The masked figure stepped closer. "Then you will see what others cannot."

They led him through a narrow alley to a small door hidden behind crates of wine. Inside, a single candle burned on a desk piled high with books. Three of them Adrian recognised immediately:

The book of the unknown:

The book of echoes: And *a third with a crimson binding* — the same one Aelius had refused to let him touch.

The masked figure removed their disguise — a woman, her hair silvered, her eyes sharp as glass.

"They were never meant to be apart," she said, her fingers brushing the crimson book. "The Unknown, the Echoes, and the Crimson Book — they are three parts of the same work. Written by the First Scribe to guide humanity through its cycles."

"Then why separate them?" Adrian asked.

"Because together, they can change a life so completely, it can alter the pattern of history. The wrong hands would rewrite the world for themselves. The Scribe foresaw this — so he scattered them across centuries, each guarded by a different line of keepers."

Adrian felt the hairs rise on the back of his neck. "And the Loveday Method?"

Her gaze settled on him. "The Method is the only way to reunite them. Without it, the books are nothing more than mirrors. With it, they are doors."

Before Adrian could speak again, the candle flickered. The woman's eyes darted to the door. "They've found us," she whispered.

A sudden pounding shook the frame. Voices shouted in Venetian outside.

She pressed the crimson book into Adrian's hands. "You must take it to the Library. Only then will it be safe. Only there will it call to the other two."

The door burst open. Dark shapes flooded the room. Adrian bolted toward the back, the book clutched to his chest.

He turned a corner — and slammed straight into the red leather chair. It shouldn't have been there, in a Venice backstreet, but it was.

Without hesitation, he sat.

The world folded, the canals vanished, and he was back in the Akashic Library. The crimson book pulsed faintly in his hands, as though it knew it was home.

Somewhere among the shelves, *The Book of the Unknown* and *The Book of Echoes* waited. And Adrian realised: once all three were together, the fourth — his own book — would finally open.

But he also knew someone else was hunting them.

Chapter Four: The Hunters in the Stacks

The Akashic Library was silent — too silent.

Adrian stood with the crimson book still warm in his hands, its cover breathing faint pulses of light. Somewhere, far down the endless aisles, something shifted. Not the gentle hum of the Library's presence, but a sharp, deliberate sound.

Footsteps. He wasn't alone.

A figure emerged from the far end of the aisle — tall, in a dark coat that seemed to absorb the light. His face was pale, the eyes cold and exacting.

"Dr. Cole," the man said without surprise, as if reading his name from the air. "You have something that belongs to us."

Adrian's grip on the crimson book tightened. "This doesn't belong to anyone. It belongs here."

The man's thin smile did not reach his eyes. "The Library is not what you think it is. Without control, it's chaos — endless lives bleeding into one another. We keep the gates closed so the unprepared don't destroy themselves... or others."

Another figure stepped into view behind him — a woman in a fitted black coat, her hair coiled tight. She spoke with quiet precision.

"The Loveday Method is dangerous in the wrong hands. We've made sure it stays hidden. Until now."

Adrian realised who they were. *The Order of the Veil.* The same organisation hinted at in the margins of Leonardo's notebooks, described as "the watchers of the gates."

"You've been guarding the Library," Adrian said.

The woman's smile was thin. "Not guarding. Deciding. Which books may be opened, and which must remain shut forever."

Adrian's chest tightened. "That's not protection. That's control."

The man's voice was like stone. "Without control, mankind will use the books to reshape reality for greed, vengeance, and power. You think we haven't seen it? We've burned whole volumes to stop it."

The crimson book throbbed in Adrian's hands. It seemed to whisper — not in words, but in a pull, guiding him deeper into the Library.

He stepped back, then turned and ran. The shelves shifted as he moved, rearranging themselves — the

Library itself helping him. He darted through a narrow passage, the sound of the Order's footsteps close behind.

Then, suddenly — the Red Leather Chair.

It waited in a shaft of pale light, older than the shelves themselves.

Adrian didn't hesitate. He sat, clutching the crimson book, and the world folded away.

When it steadied, he was no longer in the Library. He was standing on a barren plain under a sky streaked with violet clouds. In the distance, a lone stone tower rose from the earth.

Something told him this was where *The Book of the Unknown* had been hidden.

And that if the Order reached it first, the future — every possible future — would no longer belong to humanity.

Chapter Five: The Tower Without Doors

The violet sky churned slowly above the plain, its clouds twisting like ink in water.

Adrian gripped the crimson book to his chest and began walking toward the stone tower. The air here was strange — thin, as though the world itself was holding its breath.

As he drew closer, he saw that the tower had no windows. No doors. Its surface was seamless, like a single piece of carved stone rising from the earth.

And yet, the crimson book in his hands pulsed faster the nearer he came, the rhythm matching his heartbeat.

He stopped at the base of the tower. "All right," he muttered. "If you're leading me here, now would be the time to show me how to get in."

The book grew hot in his palms. Its cover split open slightly, pages fluttering though there was no wind. One page glowed brighter than the rest — a diagram, drawn in a hand older than any he'd ever seen, showing the outline of the tower and a spiral staircase *inside* it.

Beneath the drawing, words formed in a language he didn't recognise — yet somehow understood.

Only through remembrance may the walls part.

Adrian closed his eyes, focusing on the image of the tower as though he had been here before. And then... a flash. A memory that wasn't his.

He was standing in this very place, centuries earlier, wearing a cloak of white, a key of gold in his hand.

The vision faded — and the wall before him dissolved.

The interior was dim, lit by a soft golden light that had no source. Spiral stairs wound up into the darkness. At the top, on a pedestal of black marble, lay a single book bound in deep blue leather.

Even before he touched it, Adrian knew: *The Book of the Unknown.*

Its presence filled the air, thick and electric. This was the book Aelius had warned him about — the one that showed all the lives he *could* have lived but hadn't, all the roads untaken, all the alternate selves.

Beside it, on the pedestal, lay a single rolled scroll. The parchment was brittle with age, the ink a deep, rust-red. At the top was a symbol he had seen once before — etched into the frame of the Red Leather Chair.

He unrolled it carefully.

The handwriting was precise, deliberate, a guide to the readers who came after.

"To the Keeper who finds this,

I am the First Scribe. I wrote the books to guide those who wander between lives, so they might see the whole of their journey and choose with wisdom.

But knowledge without discipline destroys. That is why I created the Method — Il Metodo Loveday — the bridge between lives. Without it, the books are only mirrors. With it, they are keys to every locked door in the Library.

If you hold this scroll, you are its Keeper now. Guard it. For when the three books are together, the fourth will appear — and in it, the fate of humanity."

Adrian stared at the words, his pulse loud in his ears. This wasn't just about him. This was about *everyone*.

From far below, the sound of the tower's walls grinding open reached his ears. The Order of the Veil had found the entrance.

Adrian grabbed the Book of the Unknown and the scroll, shoving them into his satchel.

There was no Red Leather Chair here — no quick return. If he was going to make it back to the Library with the book, he'd have to get past the Order... in their world.

And judging by the sound of boots on the stairs, they were almost here.

Chapter Six: The Stairs That Weren't There

The sound of boots on stone grew louder, echoing up the spiral staircase.

Adrian's fingers tightened around the satchel. Inside, the **Book of the Unknown** felt heavier than it should — as though it carried not just pages, but worlds. The First Scribe's scroll seemed to hum faintly, like a tuning fork struck in some other dimension.

He started down the stairs two at a time.

Halfway down, the air thickened. The staircase blurred — one moment smooth stone, the next shifting into black-and-white tiles. Shadows flickered in the corners, and for a heartbeat, Adrian saw himself not as he was now, but in another life; a soldier in a forest, sword drawn, rain in his eyes.

Then it was gone.

The stairs twisted violently, and the walls melted into bookshelves stretching into darkness.

The Library. But... not the Library.

The shelves were wrong — uneven, leaning in, their books whispering in languages that scraped at the back of his mind. It was the Akashic Library *folded through a memory*.

From behind, a voice called out, sharp and cold. "Cole! Stop."

Adrian didn't. He bolted, the shelves shifting around him in a dizzying, impossible geometry. He rounded a corner and came face-to-face with the woman from the Order — her dark coat flowing behind her like a shadow made solid.

She didn't raise a weapon. She simply said, "Give us the Book. You can't imagine what it will do to you."

Adrian took a step back. "I don't think you can imagine what I'm willing to do to keep it from you."

The shelves parted, revealing a clearing of light. And there, impossibly, the **Red Leather Chair**.

It was in the wrong place, the wrong shape — part of it still blurred with the staircase from the tower — but it was enough.

He dove for it, sliding into the seat just as the woman lunged.

The world folded — but not cleanly.

Instead of the familiar stillness of the Library, Adrian landed hard on cobblestones slick with rain. He was in a narrow alley, the glow of gas lamps barely reaching the walls. The Book of the Unknown and the scroll were still with him.

Somewhere nearby, a church bell rang at midnight.

And then he realised — the clothes on his body weren't his. A long coat, a waistcoat, boots from another century.

He wasn't home. He wasn't even in his own lifetime.

And in the distance, beyond the bell's echo, he could hear the Order's footsteps. They'd followed him through time.

Chapter Seven: The Man in the Alley

Rain dripped from the edge of Adrian's hat, pooling at his collar. The cobblestones shone black under the dim glow of gas lamps. The air smelled of coal smoke and damp wool. Somewhere in the distance, the bell of St. Mary-le-Bow rang midnight.

London. Nineteenth century. He could feel it — the strange *rightness* of knowing without needing to be told. This wasn't a vision. He was *inside* a life. His body felt heavier, slower, but stronger in the arms. The clothes clung with a certain familiarity.

And then, from deep within, came a name that wasn't his. **Jonathan Hale.**

Footsteps splashed through the alley behind him. Adrian glanced back — two figures in dark coats. The Order had followed him here, their shapes barely visible through the curtain of rain.

Jonathan Hale's instincts kicked in. He turned sharply, weaving through the alleys, past shuttered shopfronts and the warm orange glow spilling from tavern doors.

But as he ran, flashes of memory surfaced — moments that didn't belong to him, yet did.

Standing in a dusty bookshop, turning the cracked spine of a leather volume. Hiding a package beneath a floorboard.

Speaking in hushed tones to a man whose face was blurred, save for the glint of spectacles. The memory pulled him like a magnet. He ducked into a narrow lane until he stood before a crooked wooden sign swaying in the rain:

"Whittaker & Sons — Antiquarian Booksellers."

The door creaked open under his touch. Inside, the smell of old paper and candlewax wrapped around him. Shelves leaned at odd angles under the weight of centuries.

In the far corner, behind the counter, sat a man in a wool vest, spectacles perched on the end of his nose. He looked up and, without surprise, said, "You've come for the Echoes."

Adrian froze. "You know?"

The man nodded. "It's been here longer than you've been alive. But you can't just take it. The Book of Echoes reveals your pattern. And if you see it before you're ready, you'll never escape it."

The shopkeeper reached under the counter and placed a small, leather-wrapped bundle on the wood. "This will take you to it — when the Library decides you're ready."

Adrian unwrapped it and found a brass key, its bow carved with three concentric circles — the same symbol etched on the First Scribe's scroll.

Before he could speak, the door slammed open. The two Order agents stood in the rain, their faces shadowed, their eyes fixed on him.

"Give us the key, Cole," the woman said. "And no one gets hurt."

Adrian slipped the key into his coat and stepped back toward the shelves. He could feel the Library pressing against the edges of this reality, waiting to pull him through again.

Somewhere, *The Book of Echoes* was calling. And now, he had the first key to find it.

Chapter Eight: The Wing of Echoes

The rain-soaked bookshop dissolved. The shelves warped, stretched, and then melted into light.

Adrian staggered back, his coat dripping, the brass key heavy in his hand. The air was no longer damp and cold but dry, thick, humming with energy. He was back in the **Akashic Library**.

But not the Library as he had first seen it.

The shelves here were taller, darker, their spines faintly glowing as if each book breathed on its own. The silence was deeper, pressing, broken only by the low thrum of something vast and alive behind the walls.

The key pulsed in his palm, warm as if alive. Ahead, set into the marble floor, was a door — not of wood or stone, but of pure shadow, a rectangle of shifting black.

Etched across its surface was the same symbol as the key: three concentric circles.

Adrian raised the key. The air locked tight in his lungs as it slid into a slot that hadn't been visible until now.

The shadow door peeled open.

Inside was a corridor lined with mirrors instead of shelves. Each one shimmered faintly, and as Adrian moved past, he saw not his reflection but lives — dozens of them.

A boy running barefoot through tall grass. A woman gripping the wheel of a ship in a storm. A soldier clutching his chest on a battlefield.

None of them were strangers. All of them were him.

At the far end of the corridor, on a pedestal of black glass, rested a single book. Its cover was plain leather, but as Adrian drew closer, it whispered — not words, but echoes of his own voice, layered across centuries.

Just as he reached out, the mirrors shivered. The air bent, and from the glass stepped a figure — tall, cloaked, its face a swirl of shifting features, flickering from one version of Adrian to another.

When it spoke, its voice was a chorus of his own, overlapping.

"You think you want the Echoes," it said. "But to see them is to know the patterns that bind you. Once you know them, you can never un-know them."

Adrian steadied himself. "Then show me. If I don't understand the pattern, I'll never break it."

The figure tilted its shifting head. "Many who asked that question were consumed by the answer."

"Maybe," Adrian said, pulse pounding. "But I didn't come this far to walk away."

The guardian stepped aside. The Book of Echoes opened on its own, pages flipping as if caught in a phantom wind. The words were not written in ink but in light — images, feelings, scenes from lives lived and lives repeated.

Adrian gasped as they filled him.

Aelric, in 10 AD, clutching a sword while his village burned.

Thomas Loveday, in 1915, drowning with the Lusitania.

Jonathan Hale, in Victorian London, clutching the brass key.

Adrian himself, now, holding all of them.

The pattern was clear — *loss, longing, the fear of being torn from home.*

He staggered, gripping the pedestal. His whole body trembled with the weight of recognition.

The guardian's voice echoed: "You see it now. The cycle you were never meant to carry. Break it... or repeat it forever."

Adrian closed the book. The pattern was real. But now, for the first time, he knew it.

And somewhere in the Library, the third and final book — the crimson one — waited for him to finish the circle.

Chapter Nine: The Crimson Truth

The echo of his other lives still rang in Adrian's chest. The Book of Echoes had shown him the pattern — a chain of fear and longing passed down through centuries. For the first time, he felt its weight not as a curse but as something he might finally set down.

But as he stood in the mirrored chamber, the satchel at his side throbbed faintly. The **Crimson Book** was inside, pulsing like a second heartbeat.

He pulled it free. Its cover shimmered darkly, as if it were wet with ink that never dried. Unlike the Echoes or the Unknown, this one did not whisper. It *waited*.

The guardian's many-faced form flickered. Its chorus voice grew hushed.

"You carry the one that was never meant to be read."

Adrian frowned. "Why?"

"Because the Crimson Book does not remember," the guardian said. "It *foresees*."

Adrian opened the cover. Instantly, the room bent — the mirrors rippled, the floor trembled.

Pages turned themselves, and visions poured out: Cities burning under a sky split by fire. Vast crowds gathering, their faces lit with hope.

The Order of the Veil standing before a great doorway of light, their hands raised not to protect it but to *seal* it shut.

And then, a final image — himself, Adrian Cole, standing at the centre of the Library, the three books open before him. Behind him, a fourth book shimmered into being, its cover blank, waiting for the first word to be written.

The Crimson Book snapped shut in his hands, as if unwilling to reveal more.

Adrian staggered. His pulse hammered in his throat. He understood now why the First Scribe had separated the books. The Unknown tempted, the Echoes revealed, but the Crimson Book... *chose.*

It wasn't a memory. It wasn't a possibility. It was destiny.

The guardian's form shifted closer, its faces flickering in and out of alignment.

"Do you see now why the Order hunts you? With all three books united, you will summon the fourth. And the fourth is not for you alone. It will write not just your story — but the story of humanity itself."

Adrian swallowed hard. "Then maybe it's not about keeping it from them. Maybe it's about writing it first."

The guardian tilted its head, its many voices almost a whisper.

"Then you must be ready to pay the cost."

A tremor shook the Library. The shelves groaned. Adrian turned — and saw them: the dark-coated figures of the Order stepping through a fracture in the air, their shapes blurred by the force it took to cross into this hidden wing.

The woman's voice rang out across the corridor. "Cole! Hand over the Crimson Book, and we may still let you live."

Adrian clutched the satchel tighter. Behind him, the pedestal still pulsed with the energy of the Echoes. In his hands, the Crimson Book glowed faintly red.

And in his mind, the image of the fourth book burned brighter than ever.

He realised, with a jolt of fear and wonder, that the final volume — his own — was no longer waiting.

It was *watching*.

Chapter Ten: The Prophecy of Fire

The hidden wing of the Library trembled as the Order advanced. Shadows lengthened across the mirrors, distorting Adrian's reflections into grotesque, warped shapes.

The woman at the front raised her hand. "The Crimson Book does not belong to you, Cole. It belongs to the Veil. We are the ones who decide which futures must be silenced."

Adrian's knuckles whitened around the book. "That's the point, isn't it? You've been deciding for us. You burn lives you think are too dangerous. You erase futures that might have saved us."

The pale man beside her sneered. "You have no idea what you're holding. Open it, and you'll see the ruin it brings."

Adrian's heart thundered. He didn't want to. Not here, not now. But the book pulsed in his hands, insistent. As though it *wanted* to be opened.

He pulled the cover back.

The mirrors exploded with light. Pages turned themselves in a frenzy, and the Library dissolved into fire.

Adrian stood on a blackened plain. Cities burned on the horizon, their towers collapsing in smoke. The sky boiled red, split by thunder. Beneath him, the ground cracked, and he saw rivers of refugees fleeing into shadow.

The Order stood nearby, watching in silence. The woman's voice echoed coldly: "There. Do you see? This is what comes if the books are joined. War. Collapse. The end of your age."

Adrian dropped to his knees, the heat searing his skin. "No... this can't be it. This can't be *all there is.*"

And then — a flicker.

Through the flames, he saw another vision overlaying the first: vast crowds standing together in sunlight, their hands raised not in fear but in unity. Children laughing as they rebuilt homes. The Library itself opening its doors to all, not just a chosen few.

Two futures. The same page.

The guardian's voice whispered in his ear, though he could not see him.

"The Crimson Book does not show what *will* be. It shows what *may* be. The future is not a sentence. It is a draft. And every soul has the right to edit it."

Adrian's pulse quickened. The Loveday Method — he understood now. It wasn't just a way to revisit the past. It was the key to re-shaping patterns across time. By healing what was carried forward, by giving back what was never his, he could lighten the chain.

The Order had it wrong. The Book wasn't a cage. It was a brush, a quill, a chance to re-write.

Adrian pressed his hand against the burning page. "Then I choose this," he whispered.

The fire stuttered, hissed, and began to fold inward. The blackened plain dissolved into grass. The collapsing cities steadied, their ruins rebuilding in fast reverse. Children's laughter replaced screams. The smoke thinned into sunlight.

The vision closed, the book snapping shut with a final thud.

When the Library returned, Adrian stood firm, the Crimson Book glowing faintly in his arms.

The woman from the Order stared at him, her face pale. "Impossible... no one can alter what is written."

Adrian's voice was steady. "Maybe not what's written? But what's chosen? Yes."

For the first time, he saw hesitation in her eyes. The pale man hissed, "You fool. You've doomed us all!"

But Adrian shook his head. "No. I've shown you the truth. The future isn't set. The Crimson Book doesn't bind us — it invites us to *choose better.*"

The air shivered. Far in the distance, he swore he heard the faint sound of pages turning — the Library itself acknowledging the shift.

And somewhere beyond the shelves, the fourth book stirred, its cover still blank, waiting for the first word of humanity's unwritten story.

Chapter Eleven: The Blank Book

The Library held its breath.

The Order stood frozen amongst the shelves, their dark coats blending with the shadows. Adrian remained at the centre, the Crimson Book clasped to his chest, its glow dimming now that the vision had passed.

But something else stirred. A low vibration, almost like the turning of a vast cog hidden beneath the floor, rumbled through the halls. Dust fell from the higher shelves. The mirrors that lined the chamber shimmered and cleared.

From the far end of the aisle came a sound he had not heard before — a page turning of its own accord.

Adrian turned. A pedestal had appeared where none had been moments earlier. And upon it lay a book larger than the rest. Its cover was pale, blank, without title or mark. The air around it shimmered faintly, as though it resisted definition.

The **Fourth Book**.

Adrian approached, his steps echoing across the marble floor. He reached out and placed a hand upon the cover. It was warm, almost alive.

The guardian's voice whispered from the mirrors. "This is what the First Scribe foretold. The Book of the Unknown shows what *might have been*. The Book of Echoes shows what *has been*. The Crimson Book shows what *could be*. But this…"

Adrian swallowed. "This shows what *will be*?"

A pause. Then: "No. This shows what you — all of you — *will write*."

Adrian pulled back slightly. "Not mine?"

"Not yours alone. No one soul may write it. It belongs to humanity itself. That is why it has remained blank. It waits for the moment mankind chooses to author its own future together."

The woman from the Order stepped forward, her face unreadable. "Do you not see, Cole? That is precisely why it must remain hidden. Give men and women the power to write the world, and they will tear it apart with their petty hungers."

But one of the younger agents behind her shook his head. "And what if he is right? What if the power is not meant to be hoarded? Haven't we seen enough ruin guarding secrets that rot instead of heal?"

The Order's unity cracked. Murmurs rippled through their ranks.

Adrian placed both hands on the blank book, speaking clearly: "This isn't about control. It's about trust. For centuries you've feared humanity's worst. Perhaps it is time to give them the chance to show their best."

The Book shivered beneath his hands. A quill of light appeared in the air, hovering above the blank page.

Adrian hesitated. He could not write this alone. To do so would only repeat the Order's mistake.

And yet, something pressed him forward. Not to finish the book. Only to begin it.

He took the quill. It moved as though guided by every life within him — Aelric of 10 AD, Thomas Loveday of the Lusitania, Jonathan Hale of London, and Adrian Cole of the present.

One word appeared, shining on the page:

Hope.

The page trembled, and the single word spread, fractal-like, becoming dozens of words, hundreds, thousands, flowing in every language. A chorus of lives, each adding to the whole.

The Book was no longer blank.

It was awake

Chapter Twelve: The Last Seizure

The word still glowed upon the page. ***Hope.***

The Fourth Book pulsed faintly, alive with the voices of countless lives, their whispers weaving through the Library like threads of light. Adrian felt it thrumming in his bones, not as a burden but as a resonance — the joining of everything he had ever been, and everything humanity might yet become.

And then, the silence shattered.

The pale man from the Order surged forward, his voice like a blade. "Enough of this folly!" He lunged towards the pedestal, his hand outstretched, veins raised on his skin as though some darker force within him strained to claim the book.

The woman did not move to stop him. Her face was unreadable, her eyes fixed on Adrian.

Adrian stepped between the man and the pedestal, clutching the satchel with the three books inside. The air grew thick, charged with the will of the Library itself.

The man snarled. "You think you can safeguard it? You, a scholar who stumbled here by accident? This power demands discipline — authority. It belongs to the Veil!"

Adrian's voice steadied, though his chest hammered. "No. It belongs to all of us. And I won't let you chain it."

The man struck — not with fist or blade, but with a force drawn from the shelves themselves. The Library groaned as if in pain, its light dimming. Shadows lashed out, whipping across the floor.

Adrian staggered, the satchel nearly torn from his grasp. The man's strength was monstrous, fuelled by centuries of stolen secrets.

And then Adrian remembered. **The Loveday Method**

It wasn't about fighting. It was about *release.*

He shut his eyes and sank into the memory of the Red Leather Chair. He felt its weight beneath him, the stillness, and the journey through lifetimes. He heard again the words he had spoken to heal Jonathan's pain: *"I will honour your memories, but I will not carry your suffering."*

Adrian drew in a long breath. The fear of failure, the guilt of centuries, the ache of every ancestor who had clung to sorrow — he felt them pressing at the edge of his being.

And he let them go.

The Library itself seemed to sigh in relief. The shadows recoiled, torn from the man who wielded them. He gasped, collapsing to his knees, his grip on the power broken.

The younger agent stepped forward, eyes wide. "It's true... he's broken the chain."

The woman lowered her gaze. For the first time, she seemed uncertain, her voice quiet. "Perhaps we were wrong. Perhaps guarding the future was never our duty. Perhaps it was only to keep it safe until this moment."

Adrian turned to the Fourth Book. The quill of light still hovered above the page, waiting. "Then help me guard it — not from people, but *for* them. This isn't mine to finish. It never was."

The Order hesitated. Some turned away, shadows of doubt flickering across their faces. Others lingered, torn between fear and the dawning sense that the world they had shaped in secret was slipping beyond their control.

The Fourth Book opened wider, its pages filling not with prophecy but with possibility. Adrian saw flashes: a thousand hands writing, painting, building; children learning without fear; generations unshackled from the trauma of those before them.

The Loveday Method was not just a technique. It was the bridge. The very act of letting go had opened the Book not to him, but to everyone.

And for the first time, the Akashic Library itself felt lighter, as though centuries of silence had lifted.

Adrian stepped back from the pedestal, the quill still glowing, and the page still alive. "The Library isn't ours to own," he said softly. "It's ours to remember. To learn from. To choose better."

The word *Hope* shone brighter, joined by a second word that appeared not from his hand, but from somewhere beyond:

"Together"

Chapter Thirteen — The Doorway of Return

The Library hummed with a strange stillness. The Order lingered in silence, scattered amongst the shadows, their faces unreadable. The Fourth Book glowed faintly, its two words shimmering like stars on parchment: *Hope. Together.*

Adrian felt its pull in his chest, as though it wished to follow him back into the world. Yet he knew instinctively it could not leave these halls. The Library held its own laws, older than time itself.

The guardian's voice rose from the mirrors, softer than before. "You have seen what was, what is, and what might yet be. But now comes the greater burden: what will you *carry back*?"

Adrian turned slowly. "You mean... whether I share it?"

"Yes. Knowledge can heal. It can also shatter. The First Scribe knew this, and so he left the choice not to himself, nor to the Order, but to each Keeper who followed."

The woman from the Order stepped forward, her voice measured. "If you tell them, you invite chaos. Faiths will crumble, governments will claw for control, and men will kill for a glimpse of the books."

The younger agent shook his head. "And if he tells no one, the suffering continues. How many more must drown beneath grief that is not theirs to bear?"

Adrian clenched his fists. He remembered Jonathan, trembling in the Red Leather Chair. He remembered the Lusitania, the screams, the anguish carried forward for generations. He thought of the Book of Echoes, showing the endless chain of repeating pain.

And then he looked at the Fourth Book. *Hope. Together.*

It had already spoken the answer.

At the far end of the chamber, a doorway of light shimmered into existence. Unlike the shadow-doors of before, this one felt calm, steady, like a breath held out for him to take.

Adrian approached. His satchel was heavy with the three books — the Unknown, the Echoes, the Crimson. They belonged here. He knew that now. Yet he also knew their wisdom had not been meant for secrecy.

He placed the satchel at the base of the pedestal. The Library seemed almost to sigh, welcoming the return.

But the Fourth Book remained open, its blank pages fluttering. One more word appeared, written in a hand he knew instantly as his own:

"Choice"

Adrian placed his hand upon the cover, whispering: "I won't tell them everything. Not yet. But I'll tell them enough. Enough to heal. Enough to give them a chance to choose differently."

The guardian's voice rumbled approvingly. "Then you have understood."

He turned to the Order, his gaze steady. "The world is changing. You can either help it grow... or be buried by the silence you keep."

Some lowered their eyes in shame. Others simply vanished into the shelves, their loyalty fractured beyond repair.

Adrian stood before the doorway of light. Behind him, the Library pulsed, eternal, infinite. Before him, the world awaited — a place both fragile and fierce, ready at last for even a glimpse of its hidden story.

He drew in a breath, and stepped through

Chapter Fourteen: Seeds of Return

The light receded, and with it the hush of the Library.

Adrian blinked, his breath misting in the cool January air. He was standing on the riverbank at Southwark, the Thames rolling darkly beneath the bridges. London lights shimmered across the water — streetlamps, office towers, the faint glow of traffic.

Ordinary. Familiar. Yet nothing could ever be ordinary again.

The satchel was gone. The books had remained behind. But their weight was still within him. The visions, the voices, the knowledge that the future was not a sentence but a page waiting to be written.

In his pocket, however, one thing remained — the brass key. It was warm to the touch, faintly pulsing, as though reminding him that the Library was never far.

Adrian returned to his flat, the quiet of it almost jarring after the immensity of the Library. He sat at his desk, staring at the empty journal before him. His hands trembled. What could he possibly write? How could he share what he had seen without being dismissed as mad, or worse — hunted by those still loyal to the Order?

And then he remembered Jonathan. The Red Leather Chair. The release.

He wrote a single line at the top of the page:

"We do not carry what is not ours to bear."

It was enough.

This was how it would begin. Not as prophecy, not as grand revelation, but as a method of healing. Quiet, human, simple; **The Loveday Method**

Weeks passed. Adrian began working quietly with those who sought him out: men and women drowning in grief they could not name, shackled by anxieties without cause. He guided them into deep trance, leading them to the Library's chair.

Some returned to the trenches of the Great War. Others to villages long turned to dust. Still others relived fears that had no words at all, only echoes.

And each time, the release came. A weight lifted. A chain broken.

Word spread, not widely, but enough. They began calling it "The Loveday Method," after one of the lives Adrian himself had once carried — Thomas Loveday of the Lusitania.

The name stuck.

One evening, as Adrian closed his journal, he looked at the city lights outside his window. He could almost feel the stirrings of the Fourth Book, far away yet tethered to him still. Its words echoed softly in his mind: *Hope. Together. Choice.*

He smiled faintly. He would not give the world the whole Library — not yet. But he could give them a way back to themselves. A way to lay down the burdens of centuries.

A quiet revolution had begun.

And somewhere, in the shadows of the city, he knew the remnants of the Order were watching. Waiting. Wondering if humanity might finally be ready for the truth they had hidden so long.

Chapter Fifteen: The Unseen Awakening

It began with a letter. A plain envelope slipped beneath Adrian's door without a stamp or postmark. Inside was a sheet of paper, covered in a stranger's handwriting:

"I don't know who you are, but last night I dreamt of a great library. There were no windows, only endless shelves. I sat in a red leather chair, and when I woke, I felt lighter than I have in years. Do you know what it means?"

Adrian read the letter three times, his pulse quickening. He had not spoken of the chair, not outside of his small circle of clients. And yet here it was — a perfect description.

He folded the paper carefully, setting it aside. Perhaps coincidence. Perhaps imagination. And yet, deep down, he knew. The Library had begun calling others.

Days later, he received another message. This one not written but spoken, whispered by a young woman who stopped him on Blackfriars Bridge.

"You've seen it too, haven't you? The books. The mirrors." Her eyes were wide, frightened yet certain. "I thought I was losing my mind until I heard your name."

Adrian guided her gently aside. "You're not losing anything," he said quietly. "You're remembering."

She gripped his hand as though drowning. "But it wasn't my life. I was someone else. A soldier, centuries ago. I died. And yet I woke."

Her voice trembled, but beneath it he heard relief. Release. The same shift he had guided others through — only she had found it on her own.

Over the following weeks, it happened again and again. Men and women he had never met came forward with their stories. Some wrote to him, some found him in the street, others sat silently across from him in cafés, waiting for him to acknowledge what they already knew.

They spoke of staircases that had no end, of doors opening onto silence, of the chair that took them into the lives of strangers who were somehow *themselves*.

Adrian realised, with a chill and a thrill in equal measure, that the Library was no longer a place he alone accessed. The boundary had thinned. Humanity itself was stirring.

But with each awakening came unease. Twice, he noticed dark-coated figures at the edges of his vision — standing too still on street corners, lingering too long in cafés. The Order had not vanished. Fractured, yes, but not destroyed.

And if others were finding their way to the Library without him, then the Order would surely try to seize them.

Adrian sat by his window late one night, the city stretched out in lights beneath him. The Fourth Book's words pulsed in his thoughts: *Hope. Together. Choice.*

It was no longer his journey alone.

The question was no longer whether humanity was ready to awaken.

It was whether they could awaken fast enough, before the Order bound them in silence once more

Chapter Sixteen: The First Circle

They met in the crypt of an old church near Clerkenwell. The stones were cold, the air damp, yet

Adrian felt it was the only place that could hold the weight of what was beginning.

Seven had come. Ordinary men and women on the surface — a nurse, a schoolteacher, a young barrister, an elderly violinist, a boy scarcely twenty, a woman who spoke little, and Adrian himself.

They sat in a circle of worn chairs. No red leather here, only wood and silence. Yet the moment their eyes met, Adrian sensed it: each had walked the staircases of the Library in their dreams, each had glimpsed lives not their own.

For a while they simply spoke. Stories spilled into the air — of forgotten battlefields, of ancient marketplaces, of hearths long extinguished. The violinist described sailing across grey seas in the body of a Norse trader. The boy trembled as he spoke of burning at the stake, the smoke still clinging to his lungs when he woke.

Adrian listened. And beneath the horror, he heard the same refrain — relief. They were no longer alone.

When the voices fell quiet, Adrian stood. "You've all been called. Not by me. Not by chance. By something older, something that waits for us to remember.

"What we do here may shape more than our own lives. The Library isn't a prison of the past — it's a doorway. And the Loveday Method is the key to using it rightly."

He looked around the circle, meeting each gaze in turn. "But with every awakening, the Order draws closer. If we continue, there will be risk. You must each decide if you will step forward, or walk away now."

The nurse was the first to nod. "I've carried fear that was never mine. And I've given it back. For the first time in my life, I feel free. I won't walk away."

One by one, the others agreed.

Together, they placed their hands in the centre of the circle. It was not a vow spoken aloud, but it bound them nonetheless.

The First Circle had been formed.

And yet, as Adrian looked at the woman who had spoken least, unease prickled through him. Her eyes did not quite meet his. Her silence was too studied, her presence too still.

When the meeting ended, and the others filed out into the foggy streets of London, Adrian lingered in the crypt. He touched the stone wall, listening to the faint hum of echoes that always seemed to follow him now.

Something was wrong.

The Library whispered faintly in his ear, a voice neither male nor female, a single word that chilled him to the bone:

"Veil."

Chapter Seventeen: The Veil Unmasked

The Circle met again a week later, this time in a disused warehouse by the docks. Adrian felt the weight of every shadow as they gathered. He tried to listen past the ordinary sounds — the creak of beams, the drip of water — for the hum of the Library that now followed him everywhere.

The woman was there again, seated at the edge of the group. Dark hair, watchful eyes, silence sharper than any word.

As the meeting began, Adrian noticed how she listened. Too closely. Not as one who learned, but as one who *recorded*.

When the boy spoke — describing how he had finally released the terror of being burned alive — the woman shifted forward, her voice cutting across the circle for the first time.

"Or perhaps," she said quietly, "these are only delusions. Dreams dressed as truth. What if the Library is nothing but a trick of the mind?"

The group stiffened. The violinist bristled. "I know what I felt. That freedom was no dream."

Her lips curved faintly. "Belief is a fragile thing. All it takes is doubt to turn freedom into madness."

The words landed like stones. Adrian saw it — the tremor in their trust, the hesitation in their eyes.

This was her task. Not violence. Corrosion. She was Veil.

When the meeting ended, Adrian caught her as the others departed. He blocked her path by the rusted door.

"You're not here to heal," he said softly. "You're here to watch us unravel."

Her gaze was cold, unreadable. "And what if I am? The Order doesn't believe humanity is ready. I was sent to prove them right."

Adrian held her stare. "And what do *you* believe?"

A flicker crossed her face. Not certainty. Something else. Something she didn't want to name.

That night, she dreamt.

Though she had not meant to. Though she had sworn she would never enter the place her masters despised.

But the Library does not bow to orders. It calls to souls, not allegiances.

She climbed the staircase. She saw the door. She stepped into the endless halls. And at the heart of it, the Red Leather Chair awaited.

She sat, trembling.

And the vision came.

A child crying in the dark, a family she had never known starving in silence, her own hands reaching not as herself, but as some ancestor long forgotten. The weight of their grief was crushing. She clutched her chest, unable to breathe — until the words Adrian had spoken echoed through her:

"I will honour your memories, but I will not carry your suffering."

She whispered to them, and the weight lifted.

For the first time in her life, she felt free.

She woke with tears on her face.

The next evening, she came to Adrian. No disguise, no pretence. Her voice was rough, as though scraped raw.

"They told me to destroy you from within," she admitted. "To scatter your Circle. I almost did. But I saw it, Cole. I saw the Library. And I... I let go."

Adrian studied her carefully. "And now?"

Her eyes glistened with something between fear and hope. "Now I believe."

Chapter Eighteen: Preparing the Circle

The Circle gathered in the crypt once more. The lamps flickered against the stone, throwing long shadows, yet for the first time Adrian felt no dread in them. There was strength here now, a quiet current binding them together.

The woman stood before them, her head bowed. No longer silent, no longer hiding.

"My name is Selene," she said. Her voice was steady, but her hands trembled. "I was sent by the Veil to undo you. To plant doubt. To see this Circle fracture before it began."

The violinist scowled, rising from his chair. "And we should trust you now?"

Selene lifted her eyes. They were rimmed red, but clear. "I saw it," she whispered. "The Chair. The lives before mine. The release. The Library is real — and the Order fears it more than they admit."

She turned to Adrian. "They know you've touched the Fourth Book. They will come for it. And if they cannot take it, they will try to silence *all of you*."

Adrian rose, looking around at the faces gathered. The nurse. The teacher. The barrister. The boy. The violinist. Selene.

"We've all seen it," he said. "We've all carried chains that were never ours. And we've all felt what it means to lay them down. That freedom — that light — is what the Veil fears. Because it cannot be controlled."

He drew in a breath. "Selene's right. They will come. But this time, we will be ready."

The boy's voice was small but firm. "What can we do? They've got power, money, and reach. We've got…" He gestured at their little circle of chairs.

Adrian smiled faintly. "We've got the Library. We've got the Method. And we've got each other. That's more than they can ever understand."

From that night, the Circle became more than a gathering. It became a school.

Adrian taught them how to enter the Library safely, how to guide themselves and others into the Chair. The nurse was the first to learn the release, then the barrister, then the violinist. Each time the chains fell, their strength grew.

Selene trained them, too — not in the Library, but in the world outside. She knew the Veil's ways, their codes, their eyes in the shadows. She taught them how to move unseen, how to listen without being caught, how to sense when danger drew near.

Together, they were no longer scattered souls. They were a Circle. A fellowship bound by memory and by choice.

One evening, as they finished their work, Selene's face darkened.

"They will not stop," she said quietly. "The Veil believes the Fourth Book belongs to them. And they will come with more than whispers. They will come with fire."

Adrian placed a hand on the journal that had become his own version of the Book. Its first page bore three words in his hand: *Hope. Together. Choice.*

He met her gaze. "Then let them come. For the first time, we are not afraid."

The Circle bowed their heads in agreement.

The storm was gathering.

But this time, they will be ready.

Chapter Nineteen: The First Strike

It came without warning.

A grey morning, London's streets slick with rain. Adrian and Selene walked together near Fleet Street, their conversation hushed, when the world around them seemed to thin.

Men in dark coats emerged from alleys, silent as shadows. Three ahead, two behind. Veil operatives — their eyes cold, their movements practised.

Adrian's pulse quickened. There was no escape this time.

The leader stepped forward, his voice low. "Cole. Selene. The Library is not yours to scatter amongst the weak. Come quietly. The Circle ends tonight."

Selene's jaw tightened. Adrian felt her shift closer, ready to fight if it came to it. But then something strange happened.

The air trembled.

Between one breath and the next, the rain seemed to hang motionless. The hum — the one Adrian always felt within the Library — now filled the street. Lamps flickered, and their reflections in the puddles rippled as though the water itself remembered.

The operatives faltered. One staggered back, clutching his chest. Another stared at Adrian with horror.

"I see them," he whispered. His face was drained of colour. "The faces... all the faces I've carried."

He fell to his knees, gasping. The others turned to him in alarm, but then it spread. One by one, their eyes glazed with visions, their composure crumbling.

They weren't attacking now. They were reliving.

The leader staggered forward, his mask of control slipping. "This... this is an illusion. It cannot be real."

But his voice shook. He saw it too. The Library had opened its doors not only to the Circle, but to the Veil themselves. It had forced them into the Chair, whether they willed it or not.

Adrian stepped towards him. "You've built your power on silence, on fear. But you've forgotten the truth: the Library doesn't choose sides. It shows what must be seen."

The man shook his head violently, but the tears streaming down his face betrayed him. "I feel it... the war, the fire... my mother's grief... It's not mine, but it's in me—"

Selene's voice cut through, calm and certain. "Then let it go. Say the words."

The man stared at her, trembling.

One by one, the operatives spoke, broken voices echoing in the rain.

"I will honour your memories, but I cannot carry your suffering…"

The air grew lighter with each release. The hum faded, the rain began to fall again.

And when it was done, the street was quiet. The operatives stood shaken, not defeated but *changed*. The doubt in their eyes was unmistakable.

The leader lowered his gaze. "If what I've seen is truth, then perhaps the Veil has been blind. Perhaps…" He faltered, swallowing hard. "Perhaps we have been guarding the wrong thing."

He turned away, his men following slowly, not as hunters but as men stripped of certainty.

Selene exhaled, her shoulders loosening. "Do you see? It's begun. Even they cannot resist it. The Library is no longer hidden. It's reaching for *everyone*."

Adrian nodded, though unease stirred within him. If the Library could reach the Veil without their consent, then its influence was spreading faster than he'd imagined.

Hope was awakening. But so too was chaos.

He whispered the Fourth Book's words under his breath. *Hope. Together. Choice.*

The battle had not ended. It had only shifted.

And now the Veil itself began to doubt.

Chapter Twenty: The Awakening Tide

For days after the confrontation on Fleet Street, Adrian felt it in the air.

London moved as it always had — taxis blaring, commuters rushing, the dull roar of trains beneath the pavements — and yet beneath it all something pulsed, subtle but unmistakable. A quickening.

It began with whispers in the Circle. The nurse reported that three of her patients had spoken of "a staircase that had no end." The barrister's colleagues muttered of doors in their dreams. Even the boy overheard strangers on the Underground describing visions of "endless shelves" and "a chair they could not resist."

Adrian listened with a mix of awe and dread. The Library was opening itself — not to a chosen few, but to *everyone.*

One evening, he found another envelope waiting on his desk. The paper was thick, foreign, the writing in a careful hand.

"Monsieur Cole, forgive my intrusion. I do not know you, but I believe you will understand. My wife has dreamt for weeks of a chair, always the same. She sits, she becomes another woman, she suffers, she releases. Each morning she wakes with tears, but also with peace. She insists this is no dream but a passage. Do you know what this means?"

The letter was unsigned.

Adrian sat back heavily. Paris. The Library's reach had crossed borders.

At their next gathering, the Circle was restless.

"It's too fast," said the violinist, his voice sharp with worry. "The Library spreads through dream after dream. What if people aren't ready? What if they see horrors they cannot bear?"

The boy shook his head. "But isn't that what we're here for? To help them release it? Maybe this is the point. Maybe it's supposed to be now."

Selene's voice was calm but grave. "Both of you are right. The release brings freedom — but the flood may drown as many as it saves. And the Veil will not sit idle. They will try to control this awakening, or twist it to their ends."

Adrian rubbed his temple, the words echoing through him. *Hope. Together. Choice.* The Library's message was clear, but the scale of it terrified him.

That night, as he lay awake, Adrian felt a pull stronger than ever before. He closed his eyes and, without climbing a stair or opening a door, found himself standing in the Library.

The guardian waited. Its form shifted, half in shadow, half in light.

"The tide rises," it said. "The Chair will no longer wait. Humanity dreams, and in dreams they will find themselves."

Adrian's voice shook. "But what if they aren't ready?"

"Readiness is a choice, not a state. Some will awaken. Some will break. That is why the Circle was born — not to stop the tide, but to guide it."

Adrian lowered his head, the truth pressing heavy on him. The Library had never intended to remain hidden. It had only been waiting for the moment the world could no longer ignore its echo.

When he awoke, the city outside his window was unchanged. But he knew — behind those lit windows, in countless homes, men and women were stirring from dreams of staircases, doors, and the red leather chair.

The Awakening had begun.

And the Circle was no longer a secret fellowship.

They were humanity's lantern in a storm the world could not yet name.

Chapter Twenty-One: The Coat of a Thousand Lives

It came to Adrian not in dream, nor in trance, but in the quiet hush of an ordinary morning.

He had been leafing through his journal when a page he had never written appeared. The ink was bold, old, yet the words were fresh as though laid there moments ago.

"The Coat of a Thousand Lives."

Beneath the title lay a passage:

"I am Kael, the First Scribe. I was there at the beginning, and I will be there at the end. You know me now by another name: Geoffrey Loveday. The circle you keep was not born of chance. The Library does only what

it was made to do: to awaken when humanity is ready. And you, Adrian, are one of its lanterns."

Adrian's breath caught. Loveday. The name whispered in the manuscripts, the name tied to the Method itself. Geoffrey Loveday — but also Kael, the First Scribe, the man who had written the Book of the

Unknown, whose words echoed in the Book of Echoes, whose life was stitched across time itself.

He saw it suddenly — the pattern.

Kael had not been bound to one age. He had worn the coat of a thousand lives, each incarnation writing a fragment of the greater design.

From the first ink scratched upon parchment to the faintest dream of tomorrow, he had been both past and future.

And now, through Adrian and the Circle, his work was ripening.

This was not chaos. Not an accident. It was the unfolding of a plan older than centuries, yet seeded within every soul before birth.

Selene entered quietly, finding him pale and trembling with the journal in his lap.

"What have you seen?" she asked.

Adrian handed her the page. She read in silence, her lips parting as the truth settled. "Then all of this... was meant?"

He nodded slowly. "The Library isn't breaking its bounds. It's fulfilling them. The Awakening is not a mistake — it is the moment Kael, Geoffrey Loveday, the First Scribe, prepared for. All of us... we wrote this into our lives before we were born."

Selene placed a hand on his shoulder. Her eyes glistened. "Then the question is not whether we can stop it."

"No," Adrian whispered. "The question is whether we can *guide it*."

That night, as the Circle gathered, Adrian spoke the truth aloud. He told them of Kael, the First Scribe, of Geoffrey Loveday. Of the Coat of a Thousand Lives.

Some wept. Some laughed. Some fell silent in awe. But all understood.

They were not fighting against a tide. They were part of it.

And the Library, at last, was doing exactly what it had always been meant to do.

The Crystal: A Touch Through Time

The Book of Echoes

A lost relic unearthed in a forgotten age.

Bound in leather that seems to shimmer like night, and clasped with iron etched in starlight, the Book of Echoes was never written by hand. Its pages are not made of parchment, but of some ancient, living fibre that pulses faintly when held.

It is said to be not a book, but a memory, whispered into form by the Crystal itself.

Each chapter tells the story of a soul who once touched the Crystal of Echoes. Some were warriors, others wanderers, some broken, some blessed—but all were called. Their stories are not written in ink, but in the very fabric of what they felt, what they healed, and what they chose to carry forward.

Each story is complete on its own.

And yet...

It is more than a collection of myths. There is a thread that binds them all.

The Crystal does not call by chance. Every soul recorded within its pages is part of a greater design—one scattered across centuries, bloodlines, continents, and realms.

These aren't just legends. They're instructions, hidden in story form. A map not of land, but of humanity's restoration.

Every myth is a key. Every choice a signal.

And when the last story is read—when the final soul is ready—the Book will unlock its final page.

A page that no one has ever read. A story yet to be written. A story... about the one holding it.

The Crystal

It is known among the ancients that many centuries ago, there lived a man with a rare gift—he could see the spirits of those who had passed. He witnessed the energy of the past shaping the flow of the future. Understanding this sacred connection, he sought to create something that could bridge the two realms.

He forged a stone made of pure crystal, imbued with ancient power.

Legend says that those who touch the crystal are transported to a secret dimension. There, they see their ancestors floating above them, whispering forgotten truths. Among them stands one figure—a mirror image of themselves. A reflection of their life.

This mirrored soul holds the key to their inherited energy—the unseen force passed down through blood and time. By facing this reflection, they release what was locked within, reclaim the strength of their lineage, and break free from the invisible chains that once bound them

The Crystal of Echoes

Long ago, before the world was divided by borders and tongues, there lived a man named Kael. He was not a king, nor a warrior, but a Seer—a walker between worlds. The villagers feared and revered him, for Kael could see what others could not: the spirits of the ancestors.

They came to him in dreams, in shadows, in the flickering of firelight. He listened to their laments, their warnings, their hopes echoing through time. He saw how the past left fingerprints on the future, how the unhealed wounds of the dead chained the living to lives not fully their own.

Burdened by the sorrow of these visitations, Kael sought a way to free his people. He climbed the highest peak of the Elara Mountains, where the stars touched the earth and the air shimmered with forgotten power. There, he fasted for nine days and nights, until the mountain answered.

From the heart of a fallen star, Kael carved a single crystal—clear as water, heavy as grief. The spirits called it **"Serentha"**, the Crystal of Echoes. It pulsed with the energy of memory, with every sorrow never spoken and every strength never claimed.

The crystal held a secret: those who touched it were not merely shown the past—they were *taken* there.

Each traveller found themselves in a realm between time, suspended in silver mist. Above them floated their ancestors—silent, watching. And in the centre, always, stood a single figure: a reflection of themselves. Not as they were, but as they were meant to be.

This reflection bore the weight of generations. It spoke with the voice of every choice never made, every gift never opened. And to those who dared to listen, it revealed the truth:

"You are not just yourself. You are every story that led to you."

In this meeting, a reckoning occurred. The traveller would feel the pain passed down, but also the power. If they embraced it—not with fear, but with understanding—the chains fell away. They would return not just healed, but awakened. And the future, once shaped by echoes, would now sing with new possibilities.

Kael passed from the world not long after creating the crystal, his purpose fulfilled. But the Crystal of

Echoes was hidden, lost to time, waiting for the ones who would need it most.

They say it still calls to certain souls—those who feel out of place, like they carry burdens that aren't their own. Those who dream of people they've never met, or cry for reasons they don't understand.

To them, the crystal whispers:

"Come. Let the past meet the present. Let the chain be broken."

Aira the Silent

The One Who Spoke Without Sound, and Sang the Storm Awake

In the parched lands of the Shifting Dunes, where the wind carved prayers into the sand, a child was born beneath a moon eclipsed. Her name was Aira, and from the moment she came into the world, she made no sound.

Not a cry. Not a whisper. Nothing.

Her village, steeped in ancient superstition, saw her silence as an omen. They believed the gods had taken her voice as a warning. So they watched her with wary eyes and offered her no place in the sacred songs of their people. Aira grew in the hush between footsteps, in the space where stories were never told.

But inside her was a storm—one that raged louder with each passing year.

She heard things others could not: the language of birds in flight, the sadness tucked beneath lullabies, the old wind that carried forgotten names across the dunes. Though her lips never moved, her eyes spoke volumes, and her silence grew heavy—too heavy to carry alone.

One day, a sandstorm rose without warning. The sky went dark, the wind screamed, and the earth disappeared beneath a wall of dust. Aira did not run. She walked into the heart of the storm, guided by a force she could not name.

There, buried beneath the sands, she uncovered a strange light—soft, pulsing, ancient. The Crystal of Echoes.

When her fingers brushed its surface, the world vanished.

She stood in a realm of silver mist, stars flickering beneath her feet, and above her—her ancestors. They floated like lanterns in the sky, glowing with memory. She looked up into their eyes and saw herself in every one of them. Then, in the centre, emerged a figure: a reflection of Aira herself, only this one *sang*.

The reflection opened its mouth, and from it came a sound so pure, it shook the realm. It was the sound of every word Aira had never spoken, every scream she had swallowed, and every song her soul had ached to sing.

The storm within her was not a curse — it was a legacy.

When she returned, she still spoke no words. But the wind bent around her with reverence. Her footsteps made music in the sand. Children who feared silence began to follow her, learning how to speak without noise, how to feel without fear.

Aira became a legend. Not for what she said — But for what she awakened in others.

The Warrior Who Could Not Win, and the Book That Remembered

Bren was born in the Kingdom of Varell, where boys were trained to wield steel before they could write their own names. His father, his grandfather, and his bloodline beyond that had all been warriors. Victory was their inheritance. Failure, a shame too great to speak aloud.

And yet — Bren lost. Battle after battle, campaign after campaign. Not from cowardice, nor lack of skill. But something always slipped—his footing, his blade, his resolve. They called him cursed. The warrior with a broken edge.

Still, he fought. Not for glory, but to prove he belonged to the line of blood he carried in his veins.

One night, after a skirmish that left more ash than answers, Bren wandered the ruins of a burned village. Rain fell hard. Blood washed into the mud. Among the rubble, he found it—half-buried beneath a shattered altar—a crystal glowing faintly, like a breath about to end.

As soon as his fingers touched it, the world pulled away.

He awoke in a realm between—no skies, no ground, only shifting shadows and distant drums like thunder from old wars. Above him floated spirits in armour, spectral blades drawn, watching him with eyes full of judgment. His ancestors.

Then came his reflection.

It stood opposite him—taller, unscarred, and proud. Its armour gleamed. Its sword was whole.

"You carry our name," it said. "But not our purpose."

"I was never strong enough," Bren whispered.

"No," the reflection said. "You were never *free*."

Suddenly, from the mist, rose a great tome—its pages endless, inscribed with symbols that pulsed like heartbeats. The **Book of Echoes.** It contained the memories of every soul who had touched the Crystal. Their stories. Their burdens. Their truths.

Bren's page was blank. "I don't belong in that book," he said.

The reflection took Bren's broken blade and plunged it into the page. The symbols flared with light. Words began to appear—not of victory, but of defiance. Not of conquest, but of compassion. He saw flashes of moments he'd forgotten—shielding a child, sparing a rival, choosing mercy.

"You were meant to break," the reflection said. "So the line could begin again."

When Bren returned, he was no longer a soldier.

He burned his armour. He reforged his blade—not as a weapon, but as a ploughshare. He built homes with his hands. He wrote his story into the earth. Others followed him—those who had fought too long, carried too much. They came with shaking hands and left with open hearts.

And in the hidden pages of the Book of Echoes, beside Kael and Aira, his story glows:

"He chose to stop the war within."

Ivenna the Watcher

The Seer of a Thousand Tomorrows and the One Path She Could Not See

"To see every path is a gift. To walk only one is a cost."

In the high cliffs of Ar'Volan, where clouds scraped the stone and thunder whispered through the bones of the mountains, lived a woman named Ivenna—the Watcher, the Oracle of Winds, the Seer Who Did Not Sleep.

From the moment she could open her eyes, Ivenna saw what was not yet.

Each choice split reality into branches. Each step, each breath, spun a new strand of possibility. When others blinked, she glimpsed futures blooming and dying in the space between heartbeats. In a single glance, she could see every version of a life—its triumphs, its tragedies, its final silence.

But what the world called a gift, she carried as a burden.

For a while Ivenna could see *all* the futures... she could live only one.

She grew hollow, haunted by the weight of possibilities—lives she would never live, loves she would never meet, children she would never bear. She stopped speaking, for every word forked into a hundred consequences. She stopped moving, lest she destroy a world by choosing the wrong step.

The villagers built her a tower of glass and sky. They brought her questions and offerings. She gave them answers, but kept none for herself. For who can choose, when every choice is both miracle and ruin?

Then, one night, as stars fell like rain across the cliffs, Ivenna saw a vision unlike any she had before.

A single point of stillness. A place beyond futures. A crystal glowing in silence.

It did not show her any paths. It *ended* them. It called not to her sight, but to her soul.

She left the tower in the night, barefoot on frost, and followed the vision across stone and silence until she found it—nestled in the heart of a cave where time did not move:

The Crystal of Echoes.

When she touched it, the visions vanished. No futures. No branches. Only a realm of stillness—mist and memory. And there, in that sacred silence, she met herself.

Not the seer. Not the oracle. Not the Watcher.

But a version of herself who had *never* seen the future.

This Ivenna was radiant—free of the weight of infinite choice, living in the wonder of the unknown. She looked at the Watcher with kindness, not pity.

"Which of us is real?" the Watcher asked.

"All of us," the reflection said. "But only *one* of us gets to walk."

Ivenna wept. Not for what she had lost, but for what she could finally become. And for the first time, she closed her eyes... and chose.

When she returned, her visions were gone.

She did not mourn them. She lived.

She learned to speak again, to dance badly, to make mistakes, to be *present*. The people called her foolish. They said her gift had faded.

But those who touched the Crystal after her... saw her page in the Book of Echoes.

"She who saw all paths... chose one."

Chapter One: The Crystal and the Echo

The woman entered the room slowly, eyes rimmed red, clutching her hands as though holding herself together. Her presence was quiet, but her pain spoke volumes before she said a single word.

"I don't think I was ever a good mother," she finally whispered.

Her voice cracked. She looked down in shame.

Guilt. Regret. Self-loathing. The weight she carried was both visible and invisible. Her energy was dim, wrapped in layers of grief.

"When I felt like this, I'd eat," she admitted. "Crisps. Chocolate. Anything. I didn't care. I stopped caring about myself."

I gently placed The Book of Echoes between us on the table. "Are you ready to remember who you truly are?" I asked.

She nodded, barely. But it was enough.

We began the journey in sacred space. Candles flickered, casting soft shadows. In the centre of the room was a glowing blue crystal, pulsating with gentle light. I placed it in her hand.

"This crystal holds a thread of your soul," I said. "It will guide you."

She closed her eyes.

Instantly, the air shifted.

In her vision, she stood in a vast stone library. The Book of Echoes appeared again, floating before her. It opened itself, pages fluttering until one stopped, glowing gold. A staircase emerged, spiralling upwards, carved from amethyst.

As she climbed, she passed people—souls—all familiar yet unknown. Some smiled. Some simply nodded. One woman touched her hand as she passed and whispered, "It's time."

At the top was a wooden door.

Her breath caught. She turned to look at me—though I wasn't physically there, I stood with her in the space between times.

"You don't have to be afraid," I said through the thread of connection.

A silver shield of light wrapped around her, summoned by the crystal's energy. She reached into her pocket—there was a key. It shimmered with stardust.

She turned it in the lock. And stepped into 1675.

She landed in a village square, her crystal still glowing softly in her palm. People walked past in clothes from another time. Then she saw herself—a woman dressed in rough linen, hair covered, carrying a baby while two little girls clung to her skirt.

Gasps echoed from the crowd.

"She's the one! The witch!"

Men in dark coats, with cold eyes and buckled shoes, stormed toward her. She screamed.

"They're taking them!" she cried. "They're taking my girls!"

A man grabbed her daughters while another held her back. "You practice witchcraft," he spat. "As punishment, your daughters will be taken."

In the background, a child—her son—stood crying. "Mama?"

Her past-self fell to her knees. "Please, take me instead."

But they were already gone.

In that moment, the woman's hand tightened around the crystal. It flared in her grasp.

A figure appeared beside her—an Elder woman cloaked in white feathers, eyes ancient as the stars. She placed her hand on the woman's shoulder.

"You have carried this sorrow for lifetimes," she said. "But it is not yours to carry anymore."

The woman sobbed.

"I thought I was a bad mother. I thought it was my fault…"

The Elder turned her toward the scene. "You were not bad. You were brave. You loved them beyond fear. You still do."

Then she turned her gaze to the woman's heart. "Let it go. Give it to the Earth. You have honoured that life. It is complete."

The crystal grew warm. It absorbed the pain like a sponge soaking up centuries of sorrow. A soft hum echoed as the light from the crystal enveloped her.

When she opened her eyes back in the healing room, her face was wet with tears—but her energy was different. Lighter. Clearer.

She looked down at the crystal in her hand. It now glowed a gentle gold.

"I remember now," she whispered. "I wasn't a bad mother. I just… lost them. I've been grieving ever since."

I nodded. "But you never lost your love. That's what lives on."

She held the crystal close to her heart.

That day, she left not just with healing—but with wholeness. The crystal remained with her, now a guide, a companion, a reminder of the strength and love that had always been hers.

Chapter Two: The Broken Voice

He came into the room with the air of someone who had spent a lifetime trying to disappear. Shoulders hunched, voice barely above a whisper. Every word felt like an effort.

"I don't know why," he said. "But every time I have to speak… in public, or even just around people, I freeze. I forget my words. My chest tightens. I feel like… I'm going to die."

I asked him if he'd ever experienced something traumatic with speaking—an argument, a confrontation, something humiliating. But nothing from this life stood out.

"It doesn't make sense," he said, frustration rising behind his soft voice. "I know I'm safe. I know no one's going to hurt me. But my body doesn't believe me."

I placed The Book of Echoes in his lap. Its golden edge shimmered faintly in the light of the nearby candle. In the centre of the room, the Crystal of Memory pulsed, soft and blue like the surface of a still lake under moonlight.

"It's not your mind that remembers," I said. "It's your soul."

He closed his eyes.

The space around him shifted instantly. The air grew colder. The candlelight flickered as a strong wind swept through the room—though no doors were open.

The Book flipped its pages on its own, stopping on one thick, parchment-like sheet. A silver key appeared beside him, and when he touched it, a spiral staircase descended from nowhere, winding downward into shadow.

He descended.

At the bottom, he found a stone corridor, lit by a single lantern.

The walls were rough and old. A sign read: France, 1942.

His breath caught.

A man in a grey wool coat met him at the end of the hall. Tall, solemn, with eyes full of knowing. He handed the young man a small, black metal box—a Morse code radio transmitter.

"You knew what was coming," the man said gently. "But you stayed anyway."

The crystal in the young man's pocket grew warmer. He looked down—its glow was brighter here, almost trembling.

Then the memories rushed in.

He was back in that body—a young man in the French Resistance. His job was to send coded messages from the forest to Allied forces. He had to be silent. Precise. Invisible.

But one night, he was found.

He remembered the boots stomping through the forest. The shouts. The cold steel of the handcuffs. The sound of fists, boots, pain.

Then, the room. Concrete walls. A single dangling bulb. And a voice demanding answers.

They asked him to give names. Locations. Passwords.

He stayed silent.

Not out of fear—but out of duty. He would not betray his people. His silence protected dozens of lives.

They beat him again. Poured water over his face. Mocked him. Starved him.

Still, he would not speak.

Until, one day, he no longer could.

The vision blurred. He fell to his knees in the memory, choking on tears and breath and terror. His present-day-self cried out, clutching his throat.

"I wanted to talk. I wanted to scream! But I couldn't... I couldn't..."

And then—someone stepped into the room.

A woman in a cloak of raven feathers, eyes like obsidian. A guide. A soul elder.

She stepped forward and placed her hands on either side of his throat, as if cradling something sacred.

"You chose silence to protect others," she said. "But you carried that silence into this life as a punishment. You forgot it was an act of love."

She looked down at the glowing crystal in his hand, which now pulsed with blue and gold.

"This crystal remembers your voice. Let it return to you."

As she spoke, the crystal melted into light, flowing like water over his throat, into his chest, wrapping around him in strands of colour and memory.

His past self—the Resistance operator—looked up. For the first time, he smiled. Not with pride, but with peace.

"I did my duty," he said softly. "I never betrayed them."

The two versions of him—the then and the now—merged.

And with that, the walls of the torture room dissolved. The war ended. Silence was no longer fear.

Back in the healing room, he gasped—and spoke.

Not in whispers.

His voice was full, warm, and steady. For the first time, he didn't stammer. He didn't fidget. He didn't freeze.

He simply spoke.

And the words came easily.

"I feel like… something's open again," he said. "Like my voice came back from somewhere far away."

"It did," I said. "From a place where silence saved lives. But now… your voice is here to heal."

He left holding the crystal in one hand, and his voice in the other.

Chapter Three: The Bride of Silence

She was the kind of woman people might call strong. Composed. Capable. Independent. But beneath her calm surface was something brittle — as if one question too personal might shatter her.

She came to me not because she was heartbroken, but because she refused to love at all.

"I can't do it," she said, folding her hands tightly in her lap. "The idea of marriage... of being chosen... it terrifies me. I panic. I shut down. I run."

There was no trauma in this life. No abusive relationships. No obvious reasons.

"It's not logical," she said. "I just feel like... I would disappear if I said yes to someone."

Her voice cracked on that word — disappear.

I placed The Book of Echoes on the altar between us. The Crystal of Remembrance pulsed with soft rose and gold light, drawing her gaze.

"This crystal," I said, placing it in her hand, "remembers the parts of you that you've forgotten — not the mind, but the soul."

The flame in the lantern beside us flared gently as she closed her eyes. The room grew quiet, as if time itself was holding its breath.

She found herself in a circular marble chamber, surrounded by pillars, silk drapes swaying in a warm breeze. The scent of roses and sandalwood floated through the air.

Before her stood a tall woman in white robes, her eyes lined with kohl, her presence regal yet tender.

"You have come to remember," the woman said. "The vow you never chose."

A glowing archway of golden vines opened behind her. The crystal in her palm shimmered and pulled her forward.

She stepped through — and became another version of herself.

The year was **72 AD**, in the hills beyond Rome.

She was young, barefoot. Adorned in fine linen and gold cuffs. But there was sorrow in her eyes. The echoes of flute music and laughter danced in the background — her wedding feast.

A man she barely knew, older and powerful, smiled at her from across the atrium. His smile never touched his eyes.

It was a political arrangement, her father's ambition secured through her obedience. Her body dressed for celebration. But her voice... her soul... locked away.

"You will smile," her mother had said sternly, adjusting her hair. "Do not embarrass this family."

Inside, she screamed. But outwardly, she bowed her head. Silent. Still.

In the vision, her present-day-self moved through the scene, invisible. She reached out to the younger her.

But the girl flinched.

"I had no choice," the younger self whispered. "If I had spoken... he would have struck me. If I had refused... they would have shamed me. I did what I had to do."

From the shadows, a young servant girl approached. She was no more than fourteen, with kind eyes and rough hands.

She turned and looked directly at the modern woman — the observer, the healer.

"You were never weak," the girl said. "You were surviving. But you do not need to live silent anymore."

Suddenly, the scene shimmered.

The young Roman bride turned to face her older self. Her lips trembled.

"I want to speak," she said. "I want to say no. I want to say yes — when I choose to."

The crystal between her hands glowed a fierce rose-gold, and a wave of sound exploded outward — not noise, but truth. It shattered the illusion of obedience like glass. The villa dissolved. The wedding vanished.

Only the two selves remained — the one who was silenced, and the one who would never be again.

They embraced. Merged. Became whole.

Back in the healing room, her eyes fluttered open. Her shoulders dropped, and for the first time, her breath came deep and full.

"I remember now," she whispered. "I wasn't afraid of love. I was afraid of losing myself in it."

She held the crystal over her heart, smiling through tears.

"But I have a voice now. And I won't give it away for anyone."

Later that week, she told me she had begun writing poetry again — something she hadn't done in fifteen years.

"I don't know if I'll ever marry," she said, "but if I do — it will be my choice. With a voice full of fire and a heart that's finally mine."

The Wanderer Who Forgot, and the Memory That Found Them

"You are not what you remember. You are what you choose to carry forward."

No one knew where the wanderer had come from.

He arrived one winter, with the snow, stepping out of the forest with no name on his lips, no past in his eyes, and no memory of who he had once been. The villagers of Kestermoor, wary yet curious, called him "Drift", for he moved like mist over the moors; quietly, without root, and always just beyond reach.

Drift could not recall a single thing before the day he appeared. Not a family. Not a birthplace. Not even the sound of his own name. And yet, he was gentle. He lit fires for the elderly, helped bury the forgotten dead. He listened, more than he spoke. He existed with grace—but without grounding.

Some called him cursed. Others whispered he was a spirit, a soul untethered.

But none knew the truth: Drift awoke every morning with a hollowness in his chest—a question so deep it echoed.

"Who was I... and why was I lost?"

And still, the greater ache was this: *What if I never find out? What if I was never meant to?*

One night, beneath a sky dusted with stars, Drift followed a strange humming wind to the old grove—where nothing had grown for years. There, nestled in the roots of a petrified tree, pulsed a faint, silver light.

The Crystal of Echoes.

It did not ask him to remember. It did not demand identity. It simply waited.

Drift placed a hand on the surface. In a moment, the world gave way.

He stood in the realm of mist, where the air shimmered with memory. But no ancestors appeared. No family tree. No great reflection of past deeds. Just silence... and a single page, floating in the air.

Blank.

This was the **Forgotten Leaf** of the **Book of Echoes**—a place reserved for those who had slipped through the cracks of history, those the world had overlooked, erased, or cast aside.

As Drift reached for it, the page began to write itself.

Not names or bloodlines, but *moments*—a hand extended to a crying child. Bread shared with a stranger. A fire lit for someone about to give up. Quiet mercies. Unnoticed kindness.

Small truths.

From the mist, a figure emerged—not someone from Drift's past, but a version of himself who had never needed to be remembered to matter.

The reflection did not ask "Who are you?"

It asked only:

"Are you ready to become?"

Drift nodded.

When he returned, the villagers found him changed—but not louder, not prouder. Just *present*. Grounded. Radiant in a quiet way.

He no longer searched for a name.

He became a guide for others who had lost their way—not to help them remember, but to help them begin.

And though no tombstone bears his name, and no scroll tells of his deeds, the **Book of Echoes** holds his page in its warmest light.

"The world may forget. But the soul remembers. And becoming… is its own kind of legacy."

The Monarch Who Chose Her Soul Over Her Throne

"To rule the world is nothing—if you lose yourself in the process."

In the sun-drenched kingdom of **Virelin**, where the sea kissed marble shores and banners danced in golden winds, a child was born to a long line of rulers. Her name was **Aelira**.

She was not the heir the kingdom expected. She was more.

Even as a girl, Aelira could hear things others could not—the cries beneath cheers, the hunger behind smiles. She sat on council steps as her father judged petitions, and though he saw paperwork, she saw pain.

By her seventeenth year, the kingdom burned from within. Greedy ministers cloaked in silk. Hungry children dying in alleys. The court praised her beauty, her poise, her "destiny". But they feared her gaze—for it saw truth.

When her father died, the crown passed to her. Aelira placed it in a chest and closed the lid.

"A throne cannot mend a soul," she whispered. "And mine is breaking."

She abandoned the palace the night before her coronation, dressed not in silk, but in shadow. The people whispered betrayal. The nobles howled disgrace. But Aelira walked alone, into the wilds beyond her kingdom, seeking not power—but peace.

For years, no one heard her name.

She lived among the forgotten—farmers, beggars, refugees. She slept beneath trees, laboured in fields, and listened to the songs of ordinary lives. And slowly, her soul, once cracked by duty and silence, began to heal.

One day, in the ruins of an old waystone deep within a forest, Aelira found it: a pulse in the ground, like a heart waiting to be touched.

The Crystal of Echoes.

When she placed her hand upon it, the mists took her.

But unlike others, she did not meet ancestors, nor a broken self.

She met a queen, standing tall in full regalia—crowned, cloaked, adored. Her reflection.

"Why did you abandon me?" the queen asked.

Aelira stepped forward. "Because you were not me. You were who they wanted me to become."

The Crystal pulsed. Around them, the echo of a kingdom flickered in light. The throne. The speeches. The illusion of glory.

And then... fire.

She saw the cost of the crown she never wore: the children she fed instead of taxing, the villages she healed instead of ruling. The queen in the reflection began to cry—not out of sorrow, but release.

"You gave up your name," the reflection whispered, "but found your soul."

And the crown melted into mist.

When Aelira returned, the world still called her a runaway. But those who met her saw something regal in her humility. Something whole. She became a silent pilgrim—an invisible monarch of the broken, the weary, and the unseen.

In the **Book of Echoes**, her page is not gold or grand. It is simple.

"She ruled no throne, but saved a kingdom. She wore no crown, but became a Queen."

The Coat of a Thousand Lives

Why I write this

When I was young, sport came effortlessly – cricket, football, anything I tried. I moved like someone born for it. People praised my skill, and saw a bright path ahead.

But each time it mattered – each trial, each moment of chance – something slipped. Something closed. An injury, a silence, a turn of fate. It was as though the universe itself said: this is not for you.

And for years, I thought I had failed.

Until I began to wonder: did I choose this path before I arrived here? Had I mapped my life from somewhere beyond, planting lessons like seeds in the dark?

Even as a child, I was called an old soul. I felt things others didn't. I knew sorrow before I knew words. I carried dreams that didn't seem mine. And still, I never imagined the road I walk now – hypnotherapist, guide, author of ten books.

It doesn't feel like I write them. It feels as if I remember them. As if something ancient is speaking through me.

These stories – these lives held within the coat – are not inventions. They are fragments of truth, stitched into fiction. They are echoes of lives still breathing through ours.

They remind us why we grieve what we've never lived. Why we flinch at shadows that aren't ours? Why do some dreams feel like memories?

We are not haunted. We are being handed something. Something to finish. Something to forgive. Something to remember.

If you feel something stir as you read, if you've always felt a pull toward the unseen – perhaps you are not just reading this book.

Perhaps it's reading you. Let us keep going. Let us remember together.

"The Soul Remembers", by Geoffrey Loveday

(Creator of The Loveday Method® and Inherited Therapy®)

You may open this book and call it fiction.

But I invite you, before you turn another page, to pause. To ask yourself "What if the stories you are about to read are not imagined, but remembered?"

Because what if you haven't stumbled onto this book by accident? What if something inside you, something older than your name, led you here?

My name is Geoffrey Loveday. For over thirty years, I have worked with those who suffer in silence. People weighed down by invisible burdens. By depression, anxiety, or grief that feels too large to explain.

And over time, I discovered something remarkable. These feelings don't always begin in this life.

In my work, I've guided people into their subconscious, not to analyse, but to remember. And what they found was extraordinary.

Lives before this one. Memories not from childhood, but from centuries long past. Emotions passed down through generations, like echoes vibrating through time. These aren't fantasy. They are the soul truth.

And The Loveday Method® is the path inward.

These stories - the Coat of a Thousand Lives, the Book of Echoes, the Enchanted Spectacles, and the Akashic Library - are drawn from the real journeys I have taken people on.

Some met themselves as midwives persecuted for healing. Others as soldiers were silenced by guilt. Still others remembered futures not yet lived. And each time, something changed.

The anxiety faded. The depression lifted. The pain made sense. Because the soul was no longer whispering, it was finally being heard.

You may still choose to call this fiction. But I ask you to consider something else. What if you are already living a story that began long before you were born?

What if the fear you feel is a message, not a flaw?

What if the sadness that comes from nowhere belongs to someone who once lived, and who now waits for you to set them free?

These are not just tales to entertain. They are doorways.

You may laugh. You may cry. You may feel an ache you cannot explain. That's how you know the remembering has already begun.

So now, take a breath. Open your heart. And let us begin the journey;

Back to where the soul first spoke. Back to the moment it all began.

But if you're still holding this book in your hands, if your heart stirred during one of the echoes, if something you couldn't explain pulled you back to read more, then

I must gently offer this: You were never just reading, you were remembering.

You see, some of us do not come here to simply live. We come carrying threads. Threads of sorrow that do not begin in this lifetime. Threads of knowing we never learned but somehow always knew. Threads of dreams we could not name, and griefs we could not explain.

And when a thread begins to hum, a soft vibration in the background of life, you don't always know where it leads. Until it leads you here.

To this page. To this breath. To this quiet remembering.

There is a word for those who feel like this. For those who remember without knowing why. For those who walk through life with one foot still somewhere else.

They are called The Threads of the Forgotten.

What are the Threads of the Forgotten?

They are not a religion. They are not a secret society. They are not chosen by ceremony or bloodline. They are born through remembering.

The moment you recognise a pain that never belonged to you, and you choose to heal it anyway; the moment you sit in silence, and the silence speaks back in echoes; the moment you realise your dreams might be memories, and your thoughts are sometimes not your own, that is when you begin the path. You are one who follows the thread.

Through lifetimes unseen, through bodies borrowed like pages in an ever-turning book, through dreams that were never dreams at all, but glimpses, whispers, truths wrapped in silence, the Thread finds you.

It does not shout. It does not rush. It hums. Softly. Steadily. Pulling you not forward, but inward. Toward the thing you have always carried but never quite named.

It winds through the ache behind joy. Through the question behind knowing. Through the longing behind breath.

And then, when the moment is right, it begins to unravel.

Not to fall apart, but to reveal.

Through The Loveday Method, you have walked these echoes. You've followed memory not with your mind, but with your heart. You've touched the seams of time itself through the weight of the Coat, through the pages of the Book of Echoes, through the vision of the Enchanted Spectacles, and what you saw there wasn't just a story.

It was you. The deeper you. The one who has done this before. Not once. Not twice. But across ages and civilisations, beneath pyramids and inside orphanages, as healer, seeker, soldier, mother, outcast, and child.

You have crossed these thresholds again and again, each time forgetting just enough to make the remembering sacred.

You've spoken in forgotten tongues. You've carried burdens that were never yours. You've died with your song still in your chest, and yet, here you are again. Alive. Awake. Aware.

And now, in this lifetime, with this breath, in this sacred moment between the seconds...

Ready to remember not who you've been, but who you were always meant to become.

Because the Thread does not lead you back. It leads you home.

Somewhere behind your story, woven between your quiet ache and your brightest you've felt it...

A hush in the air just before you speak something true. A flicker in your chest when you walk into certain rooms. The sensation that someone is watching, not with fear, but with recognition.

As if something older than memory is reaching toward you with invisible hands.

That is the Coat calling.

Not made of fabric. Not stitched with thread. But spun from the essence of lives once lived, each strand humming with echoes of what still matters.

Worn by seers and seekers, healers and hollowed-out kings, it has crossed empires, survived fire, waited in shadows, and carried the breath of forgotten generations within its folds.

And now it is calling you.

You may feel it when you least expect it, in a dream that lingers too long, a breeze that chills you on a still summer night, a feeling in your bones that you are not only you, but someone else too. Someone ancient. Someone watching through the window of your life, with quiet eyes and a half-remembered name.

Because once worn, even once, you are never the same.

The Coat does not just wrap around you. It weaves you in. You become part of the Thread. Part of the remembering. Part of the unseen story walking through time.

And the Coat?

It waits in the spaces between your doubts. It waits in silence after the question. It waits in the breath before your yes.

If you listen closely, you may hear it rustling now. Calling you. Not to become something new, but to remember what you've always been.

A keeper of lives. A bearer of echoes. A soul wrapped in time. And the Coat remembers you.

The Coat of a Thousand Lives. This is a story that must be told.

You may not have seen it. Not with your eyes. Not in the waking world. But perhaps, in your mind, your thoughts...

How "The Loveday Method" Brought One Man Back from the Edge of Life

This is more than a story. It's a testimony. A quiet miracle, made possible by presence, precision, and something deeper: a remembering of the soul.

Let's go back to 2018. We'll call him David.

David had reached a place most people only glimpse in their nightmares. He wasn't just sad, he was drowning in darkness. A silence so complete, he believed there was no way out.

One night, he stood on the edge of a building. Ready to jump. But just before he let go, a single thought interrupted:

What if I survive? What if I don't die—but live, broken, trapped?

That fear stopped him. It saved him. But only for a while.

A year later, the darkness had grown stronger. This time, he bought a rope. Drove to a secluded place. Tied the noose. Climbed the tree.

And then something impossible happened.

A stranger appeared. A man walking his dog on a route he never took. In his pocket... a Stanley knife.

He said later, "I saw it on the kitchen table this morning. Something told me to take it. I thought I'd just toss it back in the toolbox later."

He climbed the tree and cut the rope, saving David's life.

Call it coincidence. Call it fate. But that interruption was only the beginning.

A few days later, David was given a phone number. A friend said, "Just call. Once." So he did.

We spoke, and I listened. Truly listened.

Then came our first session together using The Loveday Method. And in that sacred space, something opened.

David met his grandmother. She had been gone for years, yet he saw her. Felt her arms. Smelled her perfume. He sobbed as her memory wrapped around him, not as an idea, but as a presence.

Then he saw his first birthday. His mother holding him. Not a memory, but an experience. He wasn't imagining it. He was returning.

What is The Loveday Method?

It's not hypnosis. It's not talk therapy. It is a guided, heart-centred journey, gently excavating the soul's memory. Not to fix, but to restore. To bring people back to who they were before the pain.

It's not about suggestions. It's about remembering.

Clients step into a space where time folds. Where the body reveals what words cannot. Where healing becomes felt, not forced.

David had five more sessions. Each one deeper. Each one lighter. He remembered joy. Moments of beauty hidden beneath the rubble.

Four years later, he told me: "I can still feel her hug. I don't understand it. I just know it was real."

When he told his mother what he saw, details she'd never shared, she wept.

He had remembered the unseen. And in doing so, he found his reason to live.

Today, David is not just alive. He is free.

This story is not fiction. It is living proof that some wounds are older than our names. That suffering is inherited. But so is healing.

That memory is not bound by time. That love, real, soul-rooted love, can cross lifetimes.

And that somewhere, in silence, the coat is waiting still.

The Coat of a Thousand Lives. A coat that, when worn, becomes a vessel through time, reliving a life intertwined between the past and the present.

Long before ink met parchment, before stars were named and songs were sung, there was a Coat, not crafted by hand, but born from the loom of time itself. It was said to be the First Thread.

Woven from the signs of forgotten souls and stitched with strands of lost yesterdays, the Coat of a Thousand Lives passed silently through centuries, a vessel of remembrance, a key to lives once lived binding the past to the present like a seam unseen.

To wear it was to become not only oneself, but also those whose echoes still lived in the threads. Time would fold. Moments long buried would bloom again. And the wearer would walk between then and now.

But the Coat was only the beginning.

When the world grew louder, when memory faded into myth, there came The Book of Echoes, a sentient tome whispered into existence by the final breath of a timekeeper. Its pages would write themselves in the presence of truth, recording the footsteps of those who dared to cross the veils of history.

And later, from the well of moonlight and mirrors, emerged the Enchanted Spectacles lenses through which the bearer could see what others had felt, feared, and forgotten. Not just visions, but full emotions, layers of time worn thin by understanding.

Together the Coat, the Book, and the Spectacles formed a triad of relics known only to a few: The Threads of the Forgotten. Wanderers. Witnesses. Keepers of the Unlived.

Their stories are hidden, but if you listen closely, in the silence between seconds, you might hear the soft rustle of fabric, and remember.

The Beginning: The Return of the Hidden Ones

The Universe. The Akashic Library; hidden in the folds of time itself, containing every life ever lived, or imagined, or still to come.

Together, they were guardians of the thread. But humanity forgot. Forever forgets. It only waits for you to remember.

Long before the first books were bound, before the first candle lit the dark, before time itself had settled into hours and years, there were whispers. And within them, power.

The ancients did not write as we write. They wove threads of memory, wisdom, and soul into relics that could travel without moving.

They knew one thing above all: Pain is not bound by time. Neither is healing.

And so they created tools, living tools, not to command, but to awaken. Each one carried a different vibration, a doorway into truth.

The Book of Echoes; a sentient script that writes only in the presence of remembrance.

The Enchanted Spectacles; through which you see not with eyes, but with soul.

The Crystal of Alignment; a silent conductor of memory's frequency.

The Coat of a Thousand Lives; woven from the first thread ever spun.

The Lost Key; for no door that matters opens with reason alone.

As greed grew louder, as knowledge became power instead of purpose, the ancients made a vow.

They would hide what we had not yet earned. They would protect what we no longer honoured. Until one came who would walk not for glory, but for truth.

Some say it began with a dream. Others believe it began with loss. But however it started, he remembered.

His name was Loveday. Whether that was his birth name or his echo is unclear. What is clear is this: He felt the Coat before he ever saw it. He dreamt of the Spectacles before he touched them. He heard the Book before he opened it.

He did not invent a method. He reawakened a path. The Loveday Method is not a therapy. It is an ancient inheritance, wrapped in modern breath.

It is how we find our way back to what was taken from us, or what we gave away when we forgot to listen.

And now, in this moment, as the world grows noisier than ever, the relics return.

You may find them not in temples, but in dreams. In flashes of memory that don't belong to this lifetime. In fear you cannot name. In longings that feel older than your skin.

Because the thread has begun to hum. And it knows your name.

So if you find yourself drawn to the Book, if you feel a shiver when you see the Coat, if your palms tingle at the idea of stepping into memory, you are not imagining it. You are remembering it.

The hidden ones never left. They were waiting for you. And now that you've opened this book, the journey has already begun.

Chapter One: The Scribe's Silence

Isaac had always feared speaking in public. His words caught like stones in his throat. Meetings made his palms sweat. His voice would vanish, choked by something invisible, ancient. He had no story to explain it. Only a fear too sharp to name.

Until the day the Coat found him.

Tucked behind the counter of a crumbling bookshop tucked into a forgotten alleyway in Florence, its lining shimmered oddly under the dust. "Old cloth," the shopkeeper muttered, shrugging. "It's always been here. No one ever notices it."

But Isaac did. And when he drew it around his shoulders, the world didn't spin. It shifted.

17 October, 1436 / Abbazia di San Spirito / Florence

He blinked. No longer standing in the bookshop, he was seated at a long wooden table, hunched over parchment, the scent of ink and tallow thick in the air.

His fingers, trembling, were stained with ink. His back ached from hours bent in transcription. Candles flickered low. Outside the stained-glass windows, the sun was setting behind the tiled rooftops of Florence.

He was no longer Isaac. He was Brother Tomas, a quiet, observant monk and scribe in service to the abbey. And he had not spoken a word in five years.

The room was silent except for the scratch of quills and the occasional murmured Latin prayer. Monks moved like shadows through the scriptorium, their faces pale and gaunt; their eyes wary.

Brother Matteo sat beside him, carefully copying the pages of an ancient text, Corpus Hermeticum. The teachings of Hermes Trismegistus, heretical by the Church's decree, yet too precious to be destroyed. They copied in secret, knowing discovery could cost their lives.

"Tomas," Matteo whispered once, voice barely audible. "They say the Inquisitors are close. We must finish the folios by All Souls' Day. The others are afraid."

Isaac-Tomas said nothing. He dipped his quill and continued.

Later, as night fell and the bells tolled vespers, Tomas walked the cloister garden, his cowl drawn low. He passed Brother Leon, who paused beside the olive tree where they once used to talk, before the fire, before the betrayal.

"Tomas," Leon said softly, placing a hand on his shoulder. "You haven't spoken since Luca."

Isaac's heart pounded. He remembered, not just as Tomas, but as himself. Luca. His dearest friend. The one who stood at the pulpit and spoke words of light and knowledge. The one who questioned the Church's silences.

The one they burned.

Tomas had been there. He'd watched. He'd said nothing. His silence had saved his life, and haunted every breath since. That night, he dreamed.

He stood in the courtyard again, the flames high, Luca bound and trembling. The crowd shouting "heretic." Luca looked to him, directly into his soul, and did not beg. Only said, "Remember."

And Isaac-Tomas did. He woke in his cell before dawn, heart racing, sweat on his brow. He walked to the small chapel while the others slept and lit a single candle.

And for the first time in years, he spoke. To no one in particular. To the silence itself.

"I remember."

His voice cracked. His hands shook. But something opened.

In the days that followed, he began to speak again. First in prayer, then in conversation. Then, finally, to Matteo, who embraced him with tears.

"Your voice," Matteo whispered, "it sounds like sunlight."

And Isaac realised; his voice had never been broken. It had simply been buried. In terror. In guilt. In memory.

Isaac awoke in the present. Still in the bookshop. Still holding the Coat. His heart pounded, but this time it was not with fear, but with clarity.

His silence wasn't weakness. It was a story. A life that wasn't this one, but had shaped it all the same. And now he could let it go. Because the Coat does not just bring memories. It brings freedom.

Chapter Two: The Midwife's Fire

Lila had always feared childbirth. She couldn't explain it. She wasn't a mother, and wasn't even planning to be one. But when her sister fell pregnant,

Lila began to panic. She would wake sweating in the middle of the night, images of blood and screaming caught in her throat.

Hospitals made her tremble. The smell of antiseptic made her feel faint. No doctor had answers. No therapist could unravel it.

Until the trunk arrived. A worn cedar chest, inherited from her grandmother who had passed only weeks before. Inside: lace gloves, pressed violets, a bundle of yellowed letters and a coat.

Velvet, heavy, forest green with a worn hem and a strange symbol stitched inside the collar: *Vita Memoria* – Life Remembers.

It smelled of herbs and old books. Without knowing why, Lila drew it around her shoulders. And the moment she did, she was not in her flat anymore.

She stood on a dirt path in the grey chill of early spring. Stone houses huddled together beneath a brooding sky. The wind carried the scent of rain and wood smoke.

She looked down. Her hands were calloused. A leather pouch of herbs hung at her waist. Her feet were bare and dusted with soil. She was not Lila. She was Madeleine Durand, midwife of the village of Riquewihr, nestled deep in Alsace, France in 1721.

3 April, 1721 / Alsace, Northern France

A woman screamed.

Madeleine pushed open the wooden door of a stone cottage. The birthing room was dimly lit with candles. A young woman lay on a straw-stuffed mattress, gripping the sheets, her face slick with sweat.

"Marie," Madeleine whispered gently, placing a cloth on her brow. "You are strong. Breathe with me. We are close."

Marie cried out. Her husband stood near the hearth, pale and trembling, hands twisting his hat. The birth was long. Too long.

Madeleine worked swiftly, calming the mother, easing the pain with infusions, coaxing the child into the world. And then, the stillness. The baby, a boy, was silent.

Madeleine rubbed his back. She tried everything. No breath came. Marie's scream cracked through the air like thunder. Madeleine held the tiny body to her chest, tears sliding down her face. "I'm sorry," she whispered, though she did not know to whom.

The husband stared at her in horror. And then the whispers began.

It started with murmurs. "You gave her the wrong herb." "She cursed the child." "Too many babies have been lost since she arrived."

Within hours, the village turned. The priest refused to bless the child's grave. Old women crossed themselves when she passed. And then, one night, a knock at her door.

Three men stood at her door. One with a torch. One with rope. "You will come with me," said the man with the torch. "The council has made its decision."

No trial. No questions. Just accusations. Witch.

They dragged her to the old field where herbs once grew wild. Where once she gathered healing, they now built a pyre. As they tied her to the stake, Madeleine did not fight. But she did speak.

"I only ever tried to help," she said. "Even when you didn't believe. I loved your children more than my own."

Only one face in the crowd looked away. A young girl, eyes wide with grief and knowing.

Lila gasped. The scent of fire lingered in her lungs as she opened her eyes. She was back in her apartment, on the floor, the Coat still around her shoulders.

She wept; not from fear, but from recognition. The panic she'd felt her whole life around childbirth wasn't irrational. It was a memory. A life carried forward.

She was not afraid of birth. She was afraid of being blamed for what she could not control. And now, the echo had surfaced.

And now, it could be released.

In her journal later, Lila wrote: "We carry memories we never made. We fear wounds we never earned. But once remembered, they no longer rule us."

She would go on to study midwifery. To hold space for mothers in fear. To honour the lineage of women who once healed in silence.

And every time she wore the Coat, she felt the fire again, not as pain, but as power.

Chapter Three: The Last Flight

Milo had always feared heights. Not just a tremble on ladders or a lurch in glass elevators. It was deeper, visceral.

His breath would catch, his legs turn to water. Even crossing pedestrian bridges made his chest tighten.

He didn't know where it came from. He'd never fallen. Never been in a crash. But the fear ruled him. It whispered: Don't go up. Don't trust the air. It won't hold you.

Until the night the Coat found him.

Tokyo was humming with rain that night, silver streaks slicing through neon light. Milo boarded the late train home after a shift at the emergency dispatch centre. The car was nearly empty, except for a lone coat folded neatly across the window seat.

Dark charcoal fabric, seamless lines, an emblem stitched into the collar: two wings curled around a compass rose.

No tag. No owner.

It pulsed with something he couldn't name.

He hesitated. Then, drawn by instinct more than logic, he pulled it on. And the world fractured. Wind roared in his ears.

He stood in the cockpit of a sky station, thousands of metres above Tokyo's skyline. Glass wrapped the control centre. Below, the city stretched like a glowing circuit board, cut by sky rails and floating ambulances.

He looked down at his hands, gloved, steady, and strong. His reflection shimmered on the control glass. Not Milo.

Kaito Takeda. Lead pilot for the SkyMed Crisis Response Unit.

12 May, 2049 / Future Tokyo

The city was in chaos. A cascading power surge had knocked out a third of the energy grid. Elevators failed. Smart-lights blacked out. Traffic above and below ground froze.

Kaito was directing drone ambulances from the upper platform of Tokyo's tallest tower, the Hana Spire. He barked calm orders to his AI co-pilot.

"Reroute Bravo-7 to Ward Four." "Priority on the paediatric route. The child's vitals are unstable."

There was no time to think, just act. Kaito worked with precision. He had done this before. Many times.

But then a red flash. System override.

One drone, Echo-9, the one carrying the child, disappeared from the map.

"No... no, bring it back," Kaito muttered, fingers flying across the console. "Manual override. Pull it back!"

But the drone didn't respond.

He watched, helpless, as it lost altitude, plummeting down somewhere between Shibuya and Harajuku.

Kaito was never the same. He resigned. Refused reassignment. He visited the child's parents anonymously, stood outside their home once, watching their windows in silence.

The city rebuilt. Systems improved. But Kaito did not recover.

One year later, on the anniversary of the collapse, he returned to the Hana Spire.

The cameras were off. The platform was empty. He stepped to the edge. He didn't leave a note.

Milo came back gasping. The train had stopped, the Coat still around him.

He felt sick, like he'd fallen. Like he'd watched someone else fall and couldn't stop it.

He touched his chest. His breath shook. But the fear... it wasn't of heights.

It was of failing again. Of watching helplessly. Of holding blame that time refused to erase.

Tears welled in his eyes. He whispered aloud, "I see you, Kaito."

In the weeks that followed, Milo felt different. The fear of heights didn't vanish overnight. But it changed.

He began going higher; small lifts, rooftop cafés, the sky bridge near Shinjuku.

Each time he felt the panic rise, he remembered Kaito's steadiness. His care. His humanity.

Kaito wasn't a failure. He was a man trying to save lives in a collapsing world.

And Milo, too, was learning that forgiveness sometimes travels through lifetimes, and finds you in the silence after the fall.

Some echoes rise not from what we did, but from what we couldn't change. The path forward is not to forget, but to remember with kindness.

And sometimes, to fly again.

Chapter Four: The Warning

Alina feared cities, not with a passing discomfort—but with a primal, paralyzing terror. Crowded streets made her stomach churn. She'd collapse in underground stations. Her breath would vanish in grocery aisles. The more concrete, the more noise, the more people, the smaller she became.

Her colleagues called it a severe form of social anxiety. Doctors prescribed pills and gentle exposure therapy.

But the dreams said otherwise.

She saw ashes falling like snow. Deserts where oceans had once been. Buildings drowned beneath vines. And voices whispering stories of Earth in the past tense.

She never told anyone the worst part.

In her dreams, she was never herself. She was someone else, someone who remembered.

The coat came on a Tuesday morning. No sender. No return address. Wrapped in deep green cloth and sealed with black wax.

Inside, a single note on old parchment: "Put this on when you're ready to remember."

She held it for hours before slipping it around her shoulders.

It didn't feel like clothing. It felt like permission.

Light vanished. The wind howled. When it returned, she stood in the middle of a vast silver field beneath a sky tinged lavender. Tall spires rose like coral from the horizon, flickering with embedded solar veins.

She looked down at her hands—darker skin than her own, scarred at the knuckles. Tough from work. A thin silver cuff blinked on her wrist: "Elara Noven – Earth Colony IV."

Earth was gone. What remained were colonies: floating habitats orbiting the sun, scattered settlements on terraformed moons, and domed outposts on fractured Mars. Elara lived in one of the few remaining Earth-based communities. The ground beneath her feet still bore the bones of old cities.

29 December, 2120 | Earth Colony IV

She was an eco-historian, a Keeper. One of the few tasked with remembering. Her job was to tell stories. Not myths. Not legends. But truths. Documented, recorded truths about what went wrong.

She stood in a room of children, their pale eyes wide and distant.

"...before the Rivers Cracked," she was saying, pointing to a faded image, "before the Ocean's Silence, when songs still came from whales..."

The children listened. But most didn't understand. They had never seen rain. They had never felt wind on bare skin.

One boy, no older than eight, raised his hand. "Why didn't they stop it?"

Elara blinked. That was always the question. And one she had no answer for.

Later, Elara wandered the Archive. A cavern of digital tablets and shattered books, she passed by murals, scenes from Earth's past etched with solar ink.

She paused before a wall titled The Final Fires. It showed cities burning. A great exodus. And the last ship lifting off from a coastline swallowed by the sea.

Elara pressed her hand to the mural. And suddenly she wasn't looking at history. She was in it.

The smoke. The heat. The protests turned to riots. The silence of governments as people begged to be saved. She felt the fear again.

The memory wasn't ancient. It was hers. Passed down. Encoded.

Alina opened her eyes back in her apartment. The world felt... quieter.

She looked out the window, at traffic, at crowds, at a city still humming. Not yet fallen. Her fear of people wasn't irrational. It wasn't trauma.

It was a message. She had been named Elara. She had watched the end. And now, she had come back. To warn.

She resigned from her lab. Started speaking publicly about climate trauma. Joined youth movements, not as a leader—but as a witness.

When someone asked her how she knew what would happen, she simply said: "I remember. And you can, too."

Where time touches you, every echo is a thread. Every fear a doorway. Every ache, a hidden invitation to remember, not just who you are, but who you've been. And who you're being called to become.

The Coat doesn't just take you back. It takes you where you're needed most. Sometimes, that's the past. Sometimes, it's the future. Sometimes...

It's both at once.

Chapter Five: The Temple of the Silent Star

The first time Mira touched the Coat, she felt nothing.

No flicker. No vision. Just a strange warmth in her palms and the faint scent of myrrh. She almost laughed.

But that night, when she closed her eyes, she dreamed of stars falling into the sand. Of a great golden door opening beneath her feet. Of drums echoing across stone.

And when she woke, she was not in her bed. She was barefoot, her skin dark with desert sun, her body clothed in linen robes stitched with silver moons.

763 BCE / Temple City of Eresh'Amun

The year was 763 BCE, and she was no longer Mira. She was Sa'atari, a High Dream-keeper in the Temple of the Silent Star.

The temple stood high above the salt cliffs, carved into rose-coloured stone. Sa'atari's job was not to lead rituals, but to listen to dreams.

She and others like her believed the Divine spoke not through thunder or fire, but through symbols in sleep.

The sick were brought to her. The grieving. The cursed. The shunned.

She would take their hands, look into their eyes, without a word, and close her own. And see.

Not just the surface of their pain, but the moment it began. Sometimes decades ago. Sometimes lifetimes ago.

She would return from the vision trembling, but calm. And offer a symbol. A chant. A path.

Her whispers became legend. Even kings came to kneel in the shadows of her chamber, asking "What dream am I trapped inside?"

Mira watched it all unfold, wide-eyed inside Sa'atari's body, the smells of saffron and oil, the cool rush of palm fronds brushing stone walls.

She could feel Sa'atari's heartbeat like her own. And she could feel what came next. The temple was dying.

Not from war. But from silence. A new ruler had risen. A young king obsessed with order, who outlawed dream interpretation as "madness."

He sent soldiers to the Temple of the Silent Star. To burn the scrolls. To shatter the starlit mirrors. They came at night.

Sa'atari didn't run. She stood before them, robes glowing under the moon. When they demanded she denounce her gift, she looked into the captain's eyes and simply said "You fear the dream because you've already seen your end in it."

That night, she was taken. But not before she whispered one last message to a trembling novice.

"What is forgotten in one age will be remembered in the next. Dreamers do not die. They wait."

Mira returned to herself gasping. Tears fell silently, not from sadness, but from knowing.

Her lifelong fear of sleep, the paralysis she'd battled for years, was not trauma. It was a memory. The soul's warning. A vow broken once before.

But now she could rewrite it.

She began sleeping with intention. She recorded dreams. She began helping others interpret theirs.

And one day, a young girl came to her, eyes wide with fear.

"I keep dreaming of stars falling into sand," the girl whispered. "And a woman who says the dreams aren't lies."

Mira took her hand. And the cycle began again.

Not all memories are pain. Some of it is power waiting to be reclaimed.

And through the Coat, Mira had remembered not just who she'd been, but who she had always been becoming.

The dreamer. The listener. The guide.

Because the wisdom of the soul is not lost. It is simply waiting for us to close our eyes and return.

Chapter Six: Sarah - The First Thread

Sarah had not meant to return. Not to the old house. Not to the attic. Not after the funeral. But something in the stillness of her grandmother's home called to her. Maybe it was grief. Maybe it was guilt. Maybe it was the echo of a name she could no longer say without pain; Clara.

Her best friend. Her near-sister. Gone.

Sarah found the coat folded carefully in a cedar chest beneath a drape of linen. Heavy wool. Rough seams. Timeless. She didn't remember it from childhood, and yet it felt familiar. Like something she'd been waiting for.

When she slipped it on, the attic fell away. The air changed.

1872 | Rural England

Gone was the dim dust of afternoon. In its place, the crisp scent of wood smoke, the bite of winter, the golden hush of early morning in another century.

She was barefoot. The floor was not floorboards, but cold stone. The walls were thick, plastered, and low.

And when she looked down—her hands were smaller. Paler. A ribbon of soot streaked one wrist.

Then a voice called: "Jane!"

Sarah turned, heart hammering. The name clung to her skin like dew. She ran to the window, pulling back a muslin curtain. A man in a black coat crossed the street, tipping his hat to her.

"Morning, Miss Jane," he said with a nod, as if he knew her well. Sarah managed a smile, though her heart pounded. She didn't know him, but Jane did.

Outside, horses clopped past. A cart of hay creaked by. Chimneys puffed smoke into a pink dawn sky.

She wasn't watching history. She was inside it.

Over the next hours - or days, it became hard to tell - Sarah lived Jane's life; a girl on the edge of womanhood, brimming with secrets and sorrow.

Jane sang to the fire when no one was listening. She wrote letters she never sent. She dreamed of a boy she would never marry. And she feared something, deeply; a shadow in the night, a truth never spoken aloud.

Sarah felt it all. The ache of it. The small joys. The weight of silence. But the memory that shook her came on the third night:

A scream. A barn aflame. Running. Smoke clawing her lungs.

She woke gasping, sweat-soaked, as if the fire had licked her own skin. She was not lost. Only waiting to be remembered.

The voice, Jane's voice, was everywhere now. In the creak of the stairs. The hush of the wind.

Sarah followed the thread. Piece by piece. She learned that the fire was no accident. Jane had known something. Had tried to stop it. Had failed.

And Sarah began to see herself in Jane. Another girl who had seen the signs and turned away, and who had let silence become a coffin.

To save Jane, Sarah would have to do what she never did for Clara; speak, act, listen, and REMEMBER.

When the coat finally pulled her back, she was standing in the attic once more. But she was not the same.

She touched the wool at her chest and whispered, "Not by changing the past, but by learning how to carry it forward."

And the coat, hanging on its wooden form, shimmered quietly in agreement.

Later, in her dreams, she would see a woman's face she did not recognise, a wartime painting, eyes defiant. The name "Adele" would drift across her sleep like smoke.

That night, Sarah couldn't sleep. Not after the gallery. Not after seeing Adele's eyes staring back at her from the canvas, eyes she now realised had once looked out through her own.

The street outside was quiet. Paris hushed beneath a pale moon.

She sat by the hotel window, the coat folded across her lap. Her fingers traced the seams, the edges, and the worn velvet at the collar.

She whispered the name again: "Adele."

The memory came; not as a dream, but as something deeper. A presence. A pressure behind her ribs.

She remembered the stone floors. The echo of boots in the alley. The cold bite of shame when no one would meet her gaze.

She had lived Adele. And Adele had lived a silence not unlike her own.

But Adele had written. Had painted. Had stood in the square with her head held high while the world tried to turn its back.

Sarah pressed her palm flat to the coat. She had been quiet for too long.

About Clara. About everything.

Adele had given her a gift, not just a glimpse into the past, but permission to speak. To endure. To hold the weight of a truth too long buried.

She stood. Walked to the desk. Took out a sheet of paper. She began to write.

"Clara once told me that silence could be a kindness. I believed her. But now I think silence is just a story left untold. And we owe our stories something more than that."

The coat shimmered softly in the moonlight, and Sarah knew, she wasn't done.

There were more lives in the coat. More truths waiting to be carried forward.

And this time, she would not walk away.

Not again.

Chapter Seven: The Coat that didn't Belong

It was 1920. A time when life, at least on the surface, seemed simpler. But beneath the jazz and gentility, some souls carried storms they couldn't name.

John was one of them.

By all appearances, he had everything he needed; a steady job at the rail station, a modest flat, polished shoes, and a pocket watch inherited from his father.

But inside, he felt lost. Like he was watching his own life from across the room. As if the days belonged to someone else. A quiet ache followed him, not sharp, but constant.

He had no words for it. People didn't talk about such things back then. Depression wasn't a word they used. You were just "melancholic," or "ungrateful." But John wasn't ungrateful.

He was simply out of place. A soul misplaced in time.

It started one autumn morning. John opened his wardrobe to find a coat he didn't recognise. Long, dark, heavy wool, military-style, but older. Too elegant for the war he had just returned from.

He frowned. Checked the label. There wasn't one. And yet, when he touched it, his fingers trembled.

A scent rose from the fabric. Wood smoke. Saddle leather. Something ancient.

He pulled it on hesitantly, and in that moment, the thread pulled tight. Images flooded him. Not dreams; memories.

Galloping on horseback across snow-covered fields. A woman in a velvet shawl weeping in candlelight. The weight of command. The shame of betrayal. A life that felt more like his than the one he was actually living. He dropped to his knees. Breath caught. Heart pounding. For a moment, he wasn't John.

He was Aleksandr, a cavalry officer in 18th-century Russia, disgraced after a secret uncovered, banished from everything he loved.

And he had died with regret in his chest. Regret that had passed down, waiting, until now.

John didn't know the words for what was happening. He didn't know he was part of a greater memory. That what he was feeling wasn't madness, but the echo of a soul left unfinished.

And the coat? It wasn't just fabric. It was a trigger. A relic. A tether between lives.

He would soon find the spectacles. He would soon meet a guide. And when he did, everything would change.

The next morning, John awoke feeling heavier, as if the memories from the day before had curled up in his chest and refused to leave.

He stood in the mirror, staring at the coat. It still hung neatly on the hook where he'd placed it. It hadn't moved. It hadn't changed. But somehow, it was watching him. Not with eyes, but with a presence.

He didn't wear it again. Not yet. But the images it brought wouldn't stop.

That day at the station, everything felt off. The rhythm of the trains, usually so comforting, was jagged. The way people moved, their clothes, their laughter, felt wrong. He caught himself looking for horses. Listening for Russian.

It was around three o'clock, just after the eastbound train left, when he appeared. An older man. Well-dressed, sharp blue eyes. But it wasn't his appearance that struck John, it was the feeling.

Like the man knew him. Knew something about him. Not in a suspicious way. But in a way that felt ancient.

"You've worn it, haven't you?"

The man approached slowly, hands behind his back. He didn't offer a name. Didn't introduce himself.

He simply said, "You've worn it, haven't you?"

John blinked. "I'm sorry?"

"The coat. The one that doesn't belong to this life."

A chill ran through him. He hadn't told anyone. Not a soul.

"I know how it feels," the man continued. "Like stepping into a memory that isn't yours, but somehow, it is."

John said nothing. The station blurred around them. "There's a name for what you're experiencing," the man said gently. "A way to understand it. It's called The Loveday Method."

The man handed him a small card—ivory parchment, almost warm to the touch. Embossed in gold:

The Loveday Method,

For those who carry what time has forgotten.

Ask for G. Loveday

"You may not believe in it now," the man said. "But you will. Because the past doesn't sleep forever. And you've just begun to wake up."

He tipped his hat and walked away. Gone before John could ask a single question.

That night, the dreams returned. Not Aleksandr's this time. But something deeper, older. Like flickers from many lifetimes calling his name.

And in the silence between heartbeats, he heard the whisper, "Find him. Find the one who remembers. Loveday."

John arrived at the address printed on the ivory card. It was a townhouse, tucked quietly between a row of identical buildings in Bloomsbury. Nothing about it looked unusual. But as soon as he stepped through the doorway, the air changed.

It was quieter here. Heavier, too. Not oppressive, just sacred.

A tall man with calm eyes greeted him with a warm, knowing smile. He didn't introduce himself. He didn't need to.

This was Geoffrey Loveday.

Geoffrey led John into a softly lit room. No clocks. No distractions. Only stillness.

"This won't feel like anything you've ever done before," he said calmly. "But it will feel familiar. Because the soul remembers."

John said nothing. He wasn't sure he even believed any of this. And yet, he was here.

He lay back in the chair, closed his eyes, and Geoffrey's voice began to guide him.

"With each breath," Geoffrey whispered, "you go deeper.
Not away from yourself, but into your true self."

"There's a staircase now. Ten steps. At the top, a door. When you reach it... open it. And trust what comes."

John climbed. One step at a time. And when he reached the top, he opened the door...

And Aleksandr was waiting.

He was on horseback. The cold air stung his face. Snow clung to the trees. He wore the same coat from his wardrobe.

But this wasn't London. This was Russia. His Russia.

He could feel the ache in his hands from holding the reins too tightly. He could smell the leather, the horses, and the smoke from distant fires. He could feel the shame lodged deep in his chest.

"I failed them," he said aloud. "My men. My family. I made a choice I thought was honourable, but it cost everything."

Geoffrey's voice gently floated through the memory.

"What was the choice?"

Aleksandr-John clenched his jaw.

"I spared a village. They were meant to be punished, but I couldn't. They called it treason."

John's breath caught in his real-world body. His fingers twitched. A tear slipped from his closed eyes.

"I've carried this guilt all my life, but I never knew where it came from. I've always felt like I betrayed someone."

"Even now, in this life, I never trust my own decisions. I sabotage things before they begin."

And in that moment, he saw it clearly. The echo of Aleksandr's grief was still shaping John's life.

The failure. The guilt. The exile. All of it had passed forward, unhealed. Until now.

"What does Aleksandr need to hear?" Geoffrey asked.

His voice shaking, John replied, "He needs to hear that compassion isn't weakness. That mercy isn't betrayal. He needs to be forgiven. Not by others. But by himself. He made the right choice."

And with those words, the snow began to fall slower. The cold softened. The memory began to lift.

John exhaled. Long. Deep. Like he hadn't breathed fully in years.

When he opened his eyes, he was quiet. But different. Lighter. Like something had been set down.

"It was real," he whispered. "I was him."

Geoffrey simply nodded. He had seen this before. But it never lost its magic.

"That part of you is now free," he said. "And because of that, you are free to live without his shame."

John looked at his hands. He felt them for the first time.

And for the first time in his life, he didn't feel like a stranger in his own skin.

Later, as he walked back into the city streets, John saw the world with new eyes. The coat no longer haunted him. It now felt like something that had served its purpose. A bridge to the truth.

And as he turned the corner onto Woburn Walk, he whispered to no one and everyone, "Thank you, Aleksandr. You can rest now. I'll take it from here."

Chapter Eight: The Fear That Wore a Mask

Some fears have no name. No reason. No explanation. Because they don't begin in this life. They are echoes, buried deep, waiting for the moment you're ready to face them.

It was 1943, and the world was already burning.

Raymond was twenty-six, working as a translator for the British government, helping decode intercepted French messages. His French was flawless. His instincts? Sharper than most. But there was something about him that didn't quite fit the room.

He walked like he was avoiding someone, even when he was alone. He jumped at the sound of bells. He couldn't stand the feel of silk.

"Sends a chill right down my back," he once muttered, brushing his fingers off as if something had crawled over them.

He couldn't explain it. None of it made sense. He wasn't superstitious. He wasn't dramatic. But deep down, he was terrified. Of what, he didn't know.

One afternoon, while sorting through confiscated correspondence, he found a name that stopped his breath: Lucien Delacroix.

Something about it sent a spike of cold through his spine. His hands shook. His vision blurred.

He had no memory of this man. But his body remembered.

That night, he dreamt of flames. Crowds. A wooden stage. And the sound of cheering.

But he wasn't in the crowd. He was on the stage. His hands bound. His heart was pounding. And above him, a blade.

Desperate, and quietly ashamed, Raymond sought out a man whispered about in certain circles, a hypnotist. A "memory man." Someone who helped people see things that couldn't be seen.

That man was Geoffrey Loveday.

Raymond didn't explain much when he arrived. Just that he felt something was wrong. Deeply wrong. And it had nothing to do with the war.

Geoffrey nodded, as if he'd been expecting him all along.

Under trance, Raymond's breath slowed. His fists unclenched. And the moment Geoffrey asked him to open the door, the past rushed in like a flood.

"Paris," Raymond whispered, "1789."

His voice changed. It was stronger. Sharper. Almost aristocratic.

"My name is Henri. Henri de Montreux. I'm... I'm not safe."

The images tumbled out. He had been a nobleman, not cruel, not corrupt; but marked by his bloodline.

When the revolution came, he tried to protect his staff. He tried to reason with the crowds. But it didn't matter. His name was on a list.

And one day, they came for him. Dragged him through the streets. Laughed as he was paraded in rags. Threw flowers. Spit. Applauded.

"I wasn't afraid of death," he said in trance. "I was afraid of being forgotten. Of dying a villain in a story I never wrote."

Raymond stirred. His body trembled. Tears slid down his face, unbidden.

"I've always feared being judged," he said, "for something I can't explain. Now I know why. I died misunderstood. I was made a symbol. But I wasn't the man they thought I was."

"I've carried that shame for centuries."

And suddenly, the fear that had followed him since childhood, the fear of being exposed, misread, the fear that somehow he was guilty of something unseen, made sense.

In the stillness, Geoffrey asked one question, "What would you say to Henri now?"

Raymond, his eyes still closed, smiled through the tears.

"You mattered. Your truth mattered. You were not your title. And you are remembered."

In that moment, the blade vanished, the crowd dissolved. And the fear lifted.

When Raymond opened his eyes, he took the deepest breath of his life.

"I don't feel hunted anymore," he said.

That week, he returned to work with a presence no one had seen in him before. He started speaking up. Stopped apologising. He wore silk.

He even began writing letters under a pseudonym, letters of history, of memory, of honour restored. And he signed each one "H. de Montreux".

Chapter Nine: Alan - The Forgotten Orders

His name was Alan.

The year was 1960, but his nightmares belonged to another time.

Since childhood, Alan had seen things that didn't belong to him. He dreamed of jungle heat, starvation, the metallic taste of fear. Japanese prison camps. Torture. Men dying beside him, whispering for home.

He woke up screaming more nights than not. Doctors called it anxiety. He called it a curse.

Even as the dreams faded with age, one thing remained; he couldn't bear enclosed spaces.

Crowded lifts, locked doors, windowless rooms; they triggered a terror he couldn't name. His relationships cracked under the weight of it. His wife no longer reached for his hand in the dark. His son feared the outbursts he couldn't explain.

He felt trapped in his own skin.

But Alan had always loved history. He spent his days on archaeological digs, searching for stories buried beneath the earth; lives long gone, but not forgotten.

It was during a brief trip to an old colonial guest house in the countryside, booked as part of a university excavation that everything changed.

That night, the room was quiet. The bed sheets crisp. The air still. Alan fell into a heavy sleep.

He woke to a glow. A faint shimmer in the corner of the room. He rose, heart pounding. At first, he thought it was a trick of light; moonshine through cracked shutters.

But no. There it was. A coat. Woollen. Tattered. Stained with something darker than age. And glowing faintly, like breath on glass.

He couldn't look away. He reached out. Touched the fabric. And the world fell.

1942 / Burma, Southeast Asia

When he opened his eyes, the heat hit him first. Thick, choking. Wet with rot.

His wrists were bound. Flies crawled over open wounds. Men groaned around him. Some did not move at all.

He was barefoot. He was not Alan. He was Ronald, a British commander in Burma. Captured in 1942 by Japanese forces and marched into hell.

There were no rules. No medicine. No food. No mercy.

They worked them till their bones cracked, starved them till they forgot names, beat them for speaking, for breathing, for existing.

Ronald endured. He held men's hands as they died. He buried their dog tags in secret under banyan trees. He whispered their names so they would not be forgotten.

"Don't let me vanish," one had whispered.

But he had. And now, Alan – Ronald – was back. Forced to feel it. To remember it. Not from a distance. Not from a dream. From inside.

When he returned to his body in the guesthouse, it was nearly dawn. He was on the floor, soaked in sweat. The coat lay beside him. Its seams no longer glowing. Just dark. Still. Waiting.

Alan wept. Not from fear. But from recognition.

He had lived a death not his own. A silence too deep to ignore. In the pocket of the coat, he found a note, water-stained and barely legible: "Lt. R. Whitmore. 4th Battalion. No grave. No cross. No words."

Alan stood up. His legs shook. But his mind was clear for the first time in years. He knew why the dreams had come. He knew what claustrophobia meant. It wasn't a curse. It was a memory.

And now, he would find the names. He would write them. He would speak to them. So they would never vanish again.

Two months later, Alan visited a military archive in London. While searching through burial records and POW rosters, a name caught his eye: Jakob Whitmore.

A boy listed as a wartime refugee in Europe, transported to a camp in 1942. No record of survival. Alan's breath caught. He remembered David's story. A child. A coat. A drawing.

Whitmore. Not a common name. On impulse, he searched deeper. Another name emerged: Jane Whitmore, reported dead in a fire in 1872. A village girl from Green Hollow.

The coat had not just shown them different lives. It showed them one life. Fractured. Threaded. And maybe, somehow, family.

Alan touched the coat now folded on the chair beside him. It was still. But not silent. He wasn't the only one carrying the weight of the forgotten.

And he knew he wouldn't be the last.

Anna – The Archivist's Thread (Present Day)

Anna Cartwright wasn't looking for ghosts. She was looking for lineage. A historian by training, and a genealogist by trade, Anna had made a quiet career out of reuniting people with their forgotten pasts.

Old soldier medals, family crests, lost journals, she followed names like footprints in dust.

She wasn't sentimental. Until she found the Whitmores.

It began with a request from an elderly client seeking family records tied to Green Hollow, England. A routine search.

But the names kept surfacing. Jane Whitmore. Lt. Ronald Whitmore. Jakob Whitmore.

Different countries. Different centuries. Too many deaths. Too many missing years.

Then came the strangest part; marginal notes in archived letters and war reports:

"She wore a coat, not hers." "The boy spoke of fire, but the barn hadn't burned yet." "He claimed he remembered a war not yet fought."

Anna dismissed it at first. Superstition. Confusion. Until she came across an anonymous manuscript in a London museum archive: The Coat of a Thousand Lives.

The author? Unknown. The pages? Scattered, unfinished.

But the voices – Sarah, Elijah, Lila, David, Alan – each one described the coat. A vessel. A key. A mirror of memory.

Anna felt a chill. And then she found the final entry, unlabelled but carefully folded:

"There will come a historian who sees not just the past, but the thread that binds it. If she wears the coat, she will not travel backward, but inward. She will find the origin. The first life. And the reason we were chosen."

Anna sat very still. She glanced at the coat hanging on her office door. It hadn't been there before.

Anna – The First Life (Unknown Era)

She stood before the coat for a long time. It didn't shimmer this time. Didn't pulse or whisper. It simply waited.

Anna slipped it over her shoulders.

The room tilted. Light shattered. The air spun with dust, salt, and smoke.

And then, silence. When she opened her eyes, the world had changed.

She stood on a cliff, wind in her hair, overlooking a vast and ancient sea. There were no cities. No engines. Only the hush of waves and the distant call of birds.

The sky was richer, darker. The stars were wrong. Older.

She was barefoot. Her clothes hand spun. Her fingers bore ink stains, and a satchel of scrolls hung at her side.

From behind, a voice spoke a name, "Eshara."

Anna turned. The woman who had spoken wore robes of blue and bone, hair threaded with shells.

"Come," the woman said. "The council waits."

Anna, or Eshara, followed, heart pounding. She had gone not backward. But into the beginning. Eshara was the first.

Not of the Whitmores. But of the Recorders; the memory-keepers of her people.

They did not write books. They became them. Each Recorder wore the coat during the ritual of remembrance, stitched with the lives and lessons of the ancestors.

Each wearer added a thread. A sorrow. A truth.

The coat was not magic. It was memory given shape.

Eshara's people lived by it. Died for it.

Now, the elders warned, the threads were unravelling. Too much was forgotten. Too many voices were lost.

A decision had to be made: to bury the coat forever, or send it forward. Out into time. To those who still remembered how to listen.

Anna listened.

She wandered the village. She helped harvest salt from the shore. She laughed with a boy who taught her the constellations.

And in quiet moments, she sat with the coat in her lap, tracing each stitch like a name she hadn't yet learned.

The past was not behind her. It was within her.

Before she returned, the elders gathered once more. "You were not chosen by blood," one said.

"But by the ache," another added. "The ache to remember. And to carry."

When Anna awoke, the office was just as she'd left it. But the coat was no longer on the door. It was wrapped around her.

And in the corner of her desk, freshly written in her own hand, a note: "The first thread was not sorrow. It was love. And the longing not to forget.

Chapter Ten: The Keeper

Anna stood at the window of her small London flat, the coat folded neatly beside her on a wooden chair. Outside, the city buzzed with ordinary life – buses, footsteps, laughter in cafés. None of them knew that time had bent, that history had whispered, that memory had found its vessel.

She had seen too much now to ever return to simplicity. But it was not her burden alone.

She returned to Green Hollow – the place where so many threads began. There, in the village library, she requested a meeting with the local archivist: a young man named James Whitmore.

He had always felt... different. Drawn to old stories. Haunted by vivid dreams he never understood.

When Anna entered the reading room, James stood up. He looked at her as though he'd met her in a dream.

"Have we...?"

"Not yet," Anna said softly. "But you've been waiting."

She placed the coat on the table between them. James stared at it. A pulse flickered beneath his skin – not fear, but recognition.

"What is it?"

Anna smiled gently. "It's yours now. If you choose to wear it."

He hesitated. Then, slowly, reached forward.

The coat shimmered faintly – as if the lives inside stirred to greet him.

Anna turned to go, but paused at the door.

"Remember," she said. "The coat doesn't give answers. It gives memory. What you do with it – that's the legacy."

James nodded, wide-eyed.

As Anna stepped into the street, she felt the wind pick up – soft, like the breath of time passing.

Behind her, a new story was beginning. The coat was no longer waiting. It was moving forward.

As you've turned these pages, stepping into the footsteps of those who wore the coat – Sarah, Elijah, Lila, David, Alan, Anna – I hope something stirred within you. Something deep. Something old.

A recognition. That we are all connected.

Not just by blood or name, but by memory. By silence. By the ache of stories that were never told, but somehow still live in us.

You may think the tales in this book are fiction. Neatly woven. Impossibly timed.

But I'm here to tell you, they are not. They are echoes. Reflections of lives that once were. Or perhaps still are. The coat is not just a device. It is a witness. A keeper. A call.

Each thread you followed – from the burning barn in 1872 to the jungles of Burma, from secret letters to hidden paintings – is stitched with truth. With the residue of sorrow and memory that binds us across time and silence.

Somewhere, maybe not far from you, someone is having dreams they can't explain. Visions that don't belong to them. A fear they were never taught, but feel all the same.

Maybe it's you.

Chapter Eleven: Threads Yet to Be Told

Let us now journey onward, into stories that lived long before us, and into the pain we still carry today. For in their lives, we may find the roots of our own suffering... and perhaps, the beginning of our healing.

Let us go further. Let us listen deeper.

There are more stories. More lives that once walked this earth long before; lives that still stir beneath the surface, whispering through time.

You may feel them in your quiet moments. You may sense them in your sorrow.

We are not suffering without reason. We suffer because we have inherited wounds that were never healed. We carry echoes of lives that ended in silence, voices stifled, truths buried, griefs dismissed as history.

But they were never just history. They were people. With breath. With fear. With hope.

The girl in 13th-century Spain, accused of witchcraft for dreaming in tongues she had never been taught. The healer in Ghana in 1807, who risked everything to tend to the broken while colonial boots marched closer. The boy in Manchester in 1841, who stitched buttons by moonlight but dreamed of galaxies and drew them in coal dust.

Their suffering was real. Their love was real. And we are still living the consequences, because the world does not forget what it has not faced. We bleed today for what we buried yesterday. But the coat still waits.

Not in museums or myths, but in the quiet corners of those who feel too much, cry without knowing why, dream of places they've never been.

Perhaps you, too, are one of them. And if so, the story is not finished.

It is just beginning. You are not haunted. You are being called. The coat remembers. And it is ready for you.

Chapter Twelve: The Ink That Never Dried

Some echoes are not loud. They live in the hand that hesitates. The thought that disappears before it's spoken. The knowledge we bury to protect the ones we love.

Her name now was Aiko. She lived in Kyoto, worked as a university archivist, and often said she felt more comfortable surrounded by centuries-old documents than people.

Her friends described her as graceful, precise, and reserved. She smiled often, but never for long.

Inside, Aiko felt something else. Something is missing. A quiet grief that sat in her bones like a secret.

She had no great trauma in this life. No reason to feel the ache she carried. But for as long as she could remember, she'd dreamt of ink-stained hands, calligraphy scrolls blowing in the wind, and words that were never shared.

"Sometimes I wake up mid-sentence," she said. "As if I was just about to say something important, but I never get to finish."

She found The Loveday Method through a guest lecture in England, a short workshop, more curiosity than calling.

But when she heard the phrase "healing the soul through time", she felt a shift. Not a chill, a homecoming.

She approached Geoffrey quietly after the talk.

"I think I've left something important behind," she said. "And I need to find it."

He looked at her with the soft eyes of someone who knew, who had seen this before, who had once searched for the same thing.

Under trance, her breathing slowed. The room softened. The present dissolved.

"There's mist," she whispered. "Mountains. And a house made of wood and paper."

She was no longer Aiko. She was Mei. A scholar's daughter, living in 11th-century Song Dynasty China. A calligrapher. A quiet genius.

But female.

Which meant her wisdom could only be practiced in secret.

"I wrote at night," she said. "By moonlight. Poetry. Philosophy. Questions too large for the women's quarters."

"My father knew. He taught me. But told me never to let the world know."

"He said, the world does not understand a woman who knows too much."

And so she wrote. Scroll after scroll, hidden beneath the floorboards.

Until the day they were found by a jealous official. A man who'd once courted her, and whom she had refused.

"He called me dangerous," she said, her voice trembling. "Said I mocked the Emperor with my ideas. My words were burned."

"And I was exiled, not to a place, but to silence."

In this life, Aiko had never published. Never shared her ideas aloud. She edited other people's writing with surgical brilliance, but her own voice remained in fragments.

Now, she understood why.

"I was taught that silence is honour," she whispered. "But it was fear, fear of being seen, of being erased again."

Geoffrey asked gently, "What would Mei say now, if she knew she was safe?"

Aiko's breath deepened. Her hands moved in the air, as if writing without paper.

"She would say that truth does not belong to men or women. It belongs to the soul. And she would write again."

After the session, Aiko returned to Japan with something burning in her heart. Not anger. Not sorrow. But permission.

She began writing under the name Mei-Lan a blend of who she was then, and who she is now.

Her essays, on intuition, ancestral memory, and feminine wisdom, began to ripple quietly through academia. Not loud. But impossible to ignore.

And she no longer hesitated.

Because she knew, the words she was born to speak were never truly lost. They had just been waiting.

Chapter Thirteen: The Life That Hasn't Happened Yet

Some echoes don't come from the past. Some are whispers from the future, a calling that hasn't happened, but remembers you anyway.

Her name was Leah. Thirty-two, an artist, a traveller; restless in ways she couldn't explain.

She said she had everything she needed, a stable life, a loving partner, even recognition for her work.

But something inside her refused to settle.

"It's like I'm waiting for something," she told Geoffrey. "But I don't know what. Or who. Or where."

Every night, her dreams showed her the same image, a sprawling city made of glass and light. A high tower. And a coat.

She never saw her face in the dream, only her hands. And they were always wearing the same coat. Long, dark grey, lined with something that shimmered.

She saw herself walking through corridors, guiding others, but not on Earth. At least, not the Earth she knew.

Geoffrey was quiet as he listened. Then simply said: "Some echoes don't come from behind you. Some arrive early because your soul is already walking there."

She agreed to try The Loveday Method. But she didn't want to look back. She asked, "Can I go forward?"

Geoffrey smiled gently. "Wherever your soul is ready to lead, the door will open."

Under trance, Leah stepped through the door. And what greeted her was unlike any life remembered before.

"It's... another planet," she whispered. "But it feels like home."

She described domes of soft metal and gardens grown with sound. A city suspended over the sea, powered by light and breath.

But more than anything, she described her role.

"I guide people through something called 'The Return'. They come to me when they're lost. And I help them remember who they were before they came here."

"It's like The Loveday Method. But evolved."

She was called Amari. And she wore the coat.

The same coat that once belonged to John. To Aleksandr. And perhaps, even Geoffrey.

Except now it had changed. The lining glowed faintly, embedded with shifting symbols, a living record of all who had worn it.

"I'm not just remembering her," Leah said aloud. "I am her. She's the future version of me. And she's calling me forward."

She paused. "The anxiety I've felt all my life, it's not fear. It's urgency. Because she's already waiting."

When Leah came out of trance, she didn't look disoriented. She looked clear.

She knew her life wasn't behind her. It hadn't even started. Not truly.

"The art I make, it's not random. It's part of the design. Blueprints. Visions. Pieces of what's coming."

She started creating differently. Her canvases changed. They became portals. People cried in front of them. Some said they dreamed of the places she painted, before they ever saw them.

And she no longer questioned it.

The coat, Geoffrey now realised, was not just a relic of the past. It was a marker. A mantle, worn by those chosen to carry the thread.

It had belonged to Aleksandr. It had called to John. It had waited for Leah. And it would, one day, be worn again, by those yet to be born.

Because time does not move in a straight line. It spirals. It folds. And the soul moves through it like wind through silk.

Some echoes don't come from where you've been. They come from where you're meant to go.

And when we stop trying to only heal the past, and begin listening to the future, that's when the whole timeline begins to heal.

Chapter Fourteen: David – The Thousand Lives

David was afraid to sleep.

Every time he closed his eyes, the dreams came. Not dreams. Nightmares.

Barbed wire. Trains groaning through the snow. Muffled crying in the dark. Numbers etched in blue on skin far too young. A child's hand slipping from his.

He wasn't Jewish. He wasn't even raised to believe in much of anything. But the camps haunted him like memories he never lived.

Every night, the same boy – eight, maybe ten – looked up at him as the gates clanged shut.

"Why didn't you help?"

David always woke up gasping, the sound of his own breath choking him.

He tried therapy. Meditation. Wine. Nothing dulled the dreams.

Until the day the coat found him.

It was late. The underground train was nearly empty. He sat in the corner, trying not to think, trying not to feel.

And there beside him lay the coat.

Thick wool. Old buttons. A dark lining that shimmered like ink in water.

He touched it. It was warm. Alive. He didn't think. He slipped it on.

1942 / Germany, WWII

He opened his eyes to snow. To barking dogs. To shouting in German.

He was no longer David. He was small. Hungry. Alone.

A name tag was stitched into his collar: Jakob.

David was inside the nightmare. But now it was real. He lived it.

Each day, Jakob clung to his mother's skirt. They stood in line for soup that ran out before they reached the front. They slept on wooden planks in a hut that groaned in the wind. In the mornings, Jakob would pretend he wasn't afraid – because his mother needed him to be brave.

There was a girl named Mira who braided the younger children's hair and told stories about butterflies in spring. There was a quiet man who used to be a surgeon, who bandaged fingers with torn sheets and whispered lullabies in Polish.

They were not just part of history. They were people.

They laughed when they could. They shared when they had nothing. They cried when no one was watching.

And then came the list.

Names were called. Jakob's among them.

His mother held him so tightly, he couldn't breathe. "You are loved," she whispered. "Don't forget it."

That night, he dreamed of birds flying over wire.

And then, darkness.

David woke on the floor of his flat, drenched in sweat. The coat was beside him, faintly steaming with the cold of another world.

Inside the pocket was a piece of paper, worn and torn. A drawing in pencil. A boy and a woman. Their hands touching. A yellow star on her chest.

David wept. Not from fear. Not from confusion. From knowing. From remembering.

He didn't return to work that week. Instead, he searched. He found Jakob's name in an old transport list. He found Mira's story in a single sentence buried in a digital archive.

He wrote. Not just what he saw. What he felt.

"If memory is a burden," he wrote, "it is one we carry so they don't have to."

He submitted his manuscript to a publisher. They called it fiction.

But David knew better. It was a life. One of a thousand.

And he would remember them all.

Chapter Fifteen: The Girl of Tongues

Her name was Ysabel, and from the age of seven, she dreamed in languages no one around her understood.

She would wake whispering words that sounded like wind over distant sands or sea-prayers rising from storm-swept shores. Her mother said she was cursed. Her father feared her. The village priest called it possession.

But Ysabel knew the dreams were more than madness. They were memories.

She saw a woman in a marketplace, weaving gold through silk, humming a melody long forgotten. She stood in temples scorched by war, her hands pressing ancient script into clay. She cried over a child lost to plague in a house with no walls.

The coat found her in the winter of her thirteenth year, wrapped around a merchant's relic cart, mistaken for rags. She slipped it on and fell.

Not asleep. But through.

1247 / Spain

She awoke in a quiet mountain village; older, darker, lonelier. The people spoke a tongue she knew, though she had never heard it aloud. She lived as a healer's apprentice, tending the sick and dreaming more clearly than ever before.

But fear followed her. Her gift was not welcomed. Whispers turned to stares.

A fever swept the village. Children died. And when prayers failed, blame sought a name. Ysabel.

They dragged her through the square, her coat torn from her shoulders, her mouth gagged. They called her bruja: witch.

She did not fight. She only whispered a name into the wind. Not hers, someone else's.

When Anna later discovered a scroll buried beneath a ruined chapel – inscribed in five languages, none local to the region – she knew it was Ysabel's final message.

"I was never cursed. I was remembering. Let the next who dreams speak freely. Let her not fear the fire."

Anna wept. Because she remembered the fire. And knew it was not the end.

Chapter Sixteen: The Coal Dust Dreamer

His name was Elias, and he was born with soot under his fingernails.

At nine years old, he worked twelve hours a day in a textile mill, lungs filled with lint and a back hunched from crouching under looms. The clatter of machines was all he knew. The air tasted of oil and sorrow.

He never spoke of dreams. But each night, when the others slept on straw, Elias took a nub of coal and scratched the stars he saw in his mind across the stone wall.

Not constellations he'd learned, but patterns he remembered.

Once, when the overseer caught him drawing instead of sleeping, Elias was beaten so badly he couldn't walk for two days.

But the dreams kept coming.

A telescope aimed at a sky not yet charted. A voice calling him by another name – not Elias, but Samir. A city of domes and scholars. A fire. And hands – his own – closing a book just before the flames took it.

The coat came to him during a snowstorm. Left behind on a hook in the mill yard. Wet wool. Too big. Too strange.

He pulled it on. And fell.

1094 / Córdoba, Southern Spain

He awoke in another body. Older. Taller. His hands ink-stained and calloused from writing. He stood in a study filled with scrolls, astrolabes, and star charts.

He was Samir – a scholar in Córdoba, 1094. A man hunted for the knowledge he preserved.

The city burned around him, but he would not let the maps die. He fled. Hid them beneath floorboards. Passed their patterns on through whispered teachings.

Now Elias remembered them.

He spent weeks in Samir's skin. Felt the same fear. The same defiance. He taught children in secret. He translated the stars for the illiterate. He refused to be erased.

And when the fire came again, he was ready.

Elias woke in the factory shed, trembling. His fingers still traced stars on the wall – but this time, he did not draw them alone.

Other boys came. They watched. They listened. They began to remember too.

Years later, a museum would hang one of his coal sketches beside a plaque that read:

"Anonymous, c.1841 – Thought to be one of the earliest celestial renderings from a child labourer.

Based on North African star charts believed lost in the 11th century."

The stars had found their way back.

And so had he.

The coat, folded quietly in a trunk, waited for the next child to feel too small in the world, and dare to dream beyond it.

Let us go further. Let us listen deeper.

There are more stories. More lives that once walked this earth long before us, lives that still stir beneath the surface, whispering through time.

You may feel them in your quiet moments. You may sense them in your sorrow.

We are not suffering without reason. We suffer because we have inherited wounds that were never healed. We carry echoes of lives that ended in silence, voices stifled, truths buried, griefs dismissed as history.

But they were never just history.

They were people. With breath. With fear. With hope.

The girl in 13th-century Spain, accused of witchcraft for dreaming in tongues she had never been taught. The healer in Ghana, 1807, who risked everything to tend to the broken while colonial boots marched closer. The boy in Manchester, 1841, who stitched buttons by moonlight but dreamed of galaxies and drew them in coal dust.

Their suffering was real. Their love was real.

And we are still living the consequences, because the world does not forget what it has not faced.

We bleed today for what we buried yesterday.

But the coat still waits.

Not in museums or myths, but in the quiet corners of those who feel too much, cry without knowing why, dream of places they've never been.

Perhaps you, too, are one of them. And if so, the story is not finished. It is just beginning.

You are not haunted. You are being called. The coat remembers. And it is ready for you.

Chapter Seventeen: The Weight of Stone

Her name was Arina.

In the present, she was an architect known for her precision, her elegance, and her silence.

Arina didn't cry, not even when her father died. She didn't laugh easily. Didn't allow herself to love.

What she did do was build.

Every line she drew. Every wall she raised. Every arch she designed, it was all an attempt to control something she could not name.

Until the migraines began. Unbearable. Vivid.

Each time, she saw flickers of a city on water. A girl in a crimson dress. The scent of salt and hot iron. A scream trapped in stone.

Then, during a site visit to an old Venetian palazzo, she found a coat buried beneath rubble – wool worn thin, lined with unfamiliar stitching. When she touched it, her vision blurred. And she fell.

1503 / Venice

She awoke to bells. The air brined. The alleyways close.

She was Elisabetta, daughter of a renowned sculptor. A girl whose hands were as skilled as any master's, but whose work was forbidden to be seen. Women were not allowed to chisel beauty from marble. Not allowed to sign their names.

So she created it in secret. By torchlight, beneath her father's studio, she carved angels and grief alike.

Until the day her work was discovered.

Her father claimed it was his. And the doge awarded him a commission that would last generations.

Elisabetta vanished from history. But her ache lived on.

Arina lived as her for weeks, the sorrow of being unseen settling into her bones like dust.

When she returned to her own time, she collapsed at the edge of the Grand Canal clutching a broken chisel she did not bring with her.

She began to weep for the first time in years.

And days later, she redesigned a cathedral entrance she'd been stuck on for months.

This time, she carved a single wing into the stone arch, delicate, defiant. And signed it, in the corner: "E. L."

A tribute to the girl who was never allowed to finish her masterpiece. And who had been remembered at last.

Chapter Eighteen: The Silence Beneath the Floorboards

He didn't speak until he was nearly six.

Even then, Kazuo's words came only in whispers – not of modern things, but of places he had never seen. Temples in fog. Rooms lit by paper lanterns. A garden with stones arranged like a constellation.

His parents said he was sensitive. Teachers called it a delay. But he heard music in wind chimes that others didn't, and sometimes cried when he stepped into certain rooms, as though they remembered him before he knew himself.

At seventeen, during a school trip to a Kyoto heritage site, Kazuo wandered off into a crumbling merchant house. Alone, he knelt to adjust his shoelace and felt a hollow sound beneath the tatami mat.

He pulled it back.

And there – wrapped in silk yellowed with centuries – was the coat.

The moment he touched it, his breath vanished.

1601 / Kyoto

He opened his eyes in a world of quiet grace and danger.

He was Hana, a girl trained as a geisha but burdened with a secret; she was fluent in the language of ink. Not just brushstrokes, but poetry, calligraphy, hidden messages meant for rebellion.

Her brother had died smuggling information to resistance fighters. Now she carried on his cause, in silence, in shadow, through scrolls disguised as love letters and haiku.

But the shogun's men were closing in. The walls had ears. The paper had spies.

Hana's hands were steady, but her heart bled each time she wrote a name that might die.

Kazuo, inside her skin, felt every breath, every brushstroke. The weight of silence. The threat of being seen. The yearning to speak.

And the fear that words – the very thing she loved – could cost her everything.

When the raid came, Hana hid the coat beneath the floor. She did not run. She did not beg.

She looked her captors in the eye and whispered:

"Ink outlives blades."

Kazuo woke in the present, breathless on the floor of the merchant house, still clutching the silk-wrapped coat.

He didn't speak for three days.

Then, in front of his family, he took up a brush and began to write – kanji after kanji, the strokes both ancient and his own. Poems flowed. Paintings followed.

He began teaching children with selective mutism.

Not by speech. But through ink.

On the wall of his studio, he wrote: "Every silence holds a name. Every name holds a thread."

The coat remained sealed in glass nearby, but it shimmered every time he passed, as if the silence between them still spoke.

Chapter Nineteen: The Bones of the Earth

Malik had always walked the desert like it was a question.

A geologist by training, he studied rocks, layers, and fossils. But beneath the science, something deeper pulled at him, something older.

He couldn't explain why he was drawn to places others avoided. Why the wind sometimes felt like breath. Why certain dry riverbeds made his eyes sting with grief.

His colleagues said he was eccentric. A "feeling scientist." But Malik knew he was listening to something they couldn't hear.

For years, the dreams haunted him. Visions of burning fields. Of chains biting into wrists. Of bones buried not in tombs but beneath broken tracks.

Of a name he never spoke aloud: Ayo.

It was during a dig near the Nile – meant to uncover prehistoric fish fossils – when everything changed.

He struck something soft, layered under mud and stone. Not bone. Not fossil.

Cloth.

Wrapped tight around leather. Old. Fragile. Sacred.

It was a coat.

As his fingers brushed its seam, the sky pulsed – just once – and everything went black.

1898 / Sudan

He woke to a scream.

He was barefoot, thin, and sunburned, a boy no older than thirteen. His name came not as memory, but as instinct: Ayo.

He had been taken weeks earlier in a raid. His village burned. His mother – last seen reaching for him as soldiers dragged him into the bush – never reappeared in his dreams. Only her voice. Only her song.

Now he was one of hundreds.

Forced to build a railway under British colonial command. Their purpose was war. Their bodies were fuel.

The labour was relentless. Sleep was a mercy never granted. Water was rationed like gold. Disease tore through the camp, and those who collapsed were left where they fell.

Ayo's job was to break and move stone for the tracks. He bled from his hands daily. Each strike of the pick echoed through his bones like a prayer unanswered.

But the dreams followed him here, too.

Whispers of another life, strange devices, quiet libraries, a coat that hummed like the wind.

And in the silence of night, while others whimpered or wept, Ayo remembered the stories his grandfather once told:

"The earth does not forget its dead. It sings them into the stone. That is why our feet burn when we walk over sorrow."

Ayo began to speak these stories again, in low voice, into the soil as he worked, planting memories where pain had grown.

And Malik, inside him, listened.

One night, during a dust storm, a boy named Sefu tried to escape.

He was caught. They beat him until his breath stopped.

Ayo buried him beneath the railway by moonlight, etching a single stone with the boy's name using only a bent nail.

Sefu – Still Here.

At that moment, Malik wept for the first time in years. Because it wasn't just Ayo's grief anymore.

It was his.

When he returned to the present – flung breathless into the heat of modern Khartoum – Malik didn't speak for three days.

He wandered the streets in silence, barefoot, still feeling the taste of dust on his tongue.

But the dreams had shifted.

Now he saw the faces clearly. Heard names. Remembered stories once lost to empire and time.

He founded a cultural archive – not of statues or bones, but of voices.

He visited villages. Sat with elders. Collected lullabies, grave chants, and And in every workshop he taught, he began with these words:

"We suffer today not because we are cursed. We suffer because we are carrying lives that were never allowed to finish their story."

In the corner of his archive, behind glass, the coat hangs still.

And beneath it, on a carved stone, sit five simple words: "The earth remembers for us."

Epilogue: True Threads

These are not imagined tales. They are living echoes, real lives, real people, whose transformations remind us that the past is not gone. It is waiting to be remembered, and once it is, healing begins.

Chapter Twenty: The Enchanted Mirror – A Life Remembered

How The Loveday Method Helped One Woman Reclaim Her Voice

They called her Lena. A quiet woman. Capable, kind, composed. But inside, she was drowning.

She laughed at the right times, worked hard, and cared for others. But behind her eyes lived a silence she could never name. She carried a sadness that didn't seem to belong to her.

Every relationship ended in distance. Every moment of success felt undeserved. She spoke of shame without a source. Grief with no shape.

She would later say, "It was like I was haunted, but the ghost was inside me."

Lena came to her first session reluctantly. "It's not therapy," a friend had said. "It's something different. Something deep."

She expected nothing. She sat politely. She listened.

And then, the moment came.

Her eyes closed. Her breath slowed. And something shifted, the walls of logic softened, and a memory rose.

Not a memory she could explain.

A forest. A small wooden cottage. The smell of lavender and fire smoke.

And a mirror.

Inside the mirror, she saw herself, but not as she was now. Younger. Dressed in heavy skirts. A girl with strong hands and sad eyes. She was scrubbing floors, humming an old folk song. One Lena had never heard, but somehow, knew the words to.

The girl in the mirror had a bruise on her wrist.

And a truth in her throat that had never been spoken.

The session carried her deeper.

She wasn't told the story. She felt it.

She was Margot, a servant in a country estate in 1879. Wrongfully blamed for something she did not do. Silenced. Disgraced. Sent away.

She never told anyone what happened in that house. She died in childbirth, buried in an unmarked grave.

But the echo of her story lived on. In Lena. In the pain that never made sense. In the voice she had spent her whole life suppressing.

When Lena came back from that session, she was shaking. Tears poured out; not of sadness, but of release.

She spoke for two hours straight. Not in fear. In freedom.

"It wasn't me who was ashamed. It was her. And I've been carrying it all my life. I didn't know why I couldn't trust anyone. Why I didn't believe I deserved kindness. But now... I remember. And I forgive us both."

She returned for four more sessions. Each time, a deeper thread unravelled, and her voice grew stronger.

She laughed without apology. She began painting again. She reconnected with her estranged mother – and told her everything. Not the details. The truth.

Today, Lena helps others find their voice. She volunteers at a women's shelter. And every morning, before she leaves the house, she looks in the mirror.

Not to check her reflection. But to remember the girl who once couldn't speak. And the woman who now can.

"The Loveday Method didn't give me a new life," she says. "It helped me remember the one I lost. And called me back to live it fully."

Chapter Twenty One: The Boy Who Carried a Century of Fear

Henry was born with an old name, one that felt borrowed from another era. Even as a child, his mother said he had "ancient eyes."

He never played like the others. He asked questions about death before he knew how to spell the word.

From the age of five, he woke in terror, heart racing, throat tight, dreams full of smoke and steel. His parents called them night terrors. Doctors tried their best.

At school, he was bright but distant. At home, he would sit at windows during storms, whispering things he couldn't explain; prayers in a language no one taught him.

By twenty, he'd learned to mask it. But he still carried that feeling: "I don't belong here."

It was a winter evening in 2046. London was slick with rain. Henry ducked into an old shop for shelter – the kind of place that looked like it had been forgotten by time.

The sign above was so faded it was unreadable. Inside, it smelled of wax, smoke, and something almost like rosemary.

The man behind the counter was middle-aged, dressed in a waistcoat and tie; old-fashioned, elegant, and calm.

"You look frozen," he said, eyes twinkling. "Soup?"

Henry nodded, grateful.

As the warmth spread through him, he noticed the shop more closely. It wasn't just old – it was wrong for the time. Lanterns glowed instead of lights. Books with leather spines lined the walls. A single ticking clock hung above a velvet curtain.

Then he saw it – in the far corner: a tiny door. No more than a metre high.

It creaked open, though no one had touched it. Something shimmered behind it. Henry stepped through.

The coat was waiting.

It was impossibly old. Dusty, frayed, yet humming with something alive. The moment he touched it, it wrapped around him – not with fabric, but with recognition.

He didn't fall. He remembered.

1327 / England

A monastery. Stone walls. Candlelight. Cold.

He was Brother Henricus, a monk in his early thirties, quiet, brilliant, and deeply afraid. Not of God. Not of war.

But of truth.

Henricus had once healed with herbs, with words, with compassion. But he had seen too much torture disguised as faith, too much cruelty justified by dogma.

He had witnessed his friend, Brother Theo, taken and burned for what they called heresy. His crime? Speaking Latin words that questioned the Church's control over fear.

And Henricus had said nothing. He had watched. Then turned away.

For years, he buried it in silence. But the guilt became illness. The fear turned to trembling. And the body began to wither.

He died of "madness," they said. But it was memory that killed him.

Henry felt every heartbeat. Every lash of guilt. Every scream that Henricus could not silence.

And in one moment – one aching, final act – he saw himself kneeling by the fire, writing Theo's name into the margins of a sacred book. Hiding it. Preserving it.

"Let one soul remember him."

And Henry, now back in his own body, whispered:

"I remember."

He woke back in the shop. The door was gone. The coat hanging quietly behind glass.

The man at the counter only smiled. "You made it back."

Henry left the shop with his chest open like never before. He felt the same. And entirely different.

The panic attacks lessened. The dreams shifted. He no longer feared death.

Because he now knew he had already lived and carried a fear that was never truly his.

Today, Henry studies medieval history. He translates forgotten texts. And in every margin, he writes a single name: Theo.

"We are the voice for those who were silenced. Their fears live in us, until we choose to free them."

Chapter Twenty Two: The One Who Knew His Name

There are moments when the soul stops walking in one direction. Moments when time folds quietly and the past looks into the eyes of the future. And they both whisper the same name.

It had been weeks since Geoffrey guided Leah through her future life. Weeks since the image of the coat, glowing with remembered lives, refused to leave him.

He could still see her, Amari, walking corridors of light, guiding souls through what she called The Return. And when he looked into Leah's eyes that day, he wasn't just looking at her future.

He was looking at his own. Not in form, but in meaning.

The Book had changed, too. It pulsed differently now. It no longer revealed only the past, but began offering glimpses of what was unfolding ahead.

Sometimes, Geoffrey would hear whispers during sessions that hadn't yet occurred. See symbols no one had drawn. Feel the presence of someone nearby, just beyond the veil.

Someone familiar. Someone... watching.

It was raining when the young man arrived.

He was no more than twenty-one. His coat was soaked. His accent was unfamiliar. But he carried something ancient in his eyes, and something impossible in his words.

He didn't knock. He just waited, quietly, outside Geoffrey's door, as though he had been expected.

Geoffrey opened it. And the man smiled.

"It's good to see you again, Alarion."

Geoffrey froze.

Only two people had ever called him that name. Both had been in trance. Both had been in lifetimes hundreds, sometimes thousands of years apart.

"Who are you?" he asked quietly.

The young man stepped inside, looking around the room. His eyes softened as they landed on the Book.

"My name is Cassian," he said. "I came through your teachings, but not from here. Not from this time."

He placed a small device – round, smooth, humming lightly – on the table.

"You wrote about it," he said. "In the Archive. In the Library of Light. I followed your work for years before I found you."

Geoffrey's mouth went dry. "But I haven't written that yet."

Cassian only smiled. "Not yet. But you will. Because I read it."

He wasn't from the past. He wasn't from now. He was a seeker from the future, one shaped by Geoffrey's legacy, who had returned to awaken the final truth; that the healer was not just remembering past lives, he was living in the beginning of something that would change the way souls moved through time itself.

That night, Geoffrey sat in silence.

The rain fell. The Book glowed faintly. And he realised he had become the echo.

The echo someone else would follow. The one whose story would ripple forward, and whose words would be remembered before they were ever written.

And in that silence, the Book finally turned its last page. Not to close the story, but to begin a new one.

Some echoes reach backward. Some spiral forward. But the rarest of all are the ones that meet themselves, and remember who they came here to be.

Chapter Twenty Three: The Keeper's Return

Some seekers are not born in the past. They are born in the echoes of the legacy you haven't written yet, drawn to the moment where it all began.

Cassian stood quietly in Geoffrey's study, his fingers lightly brushing the surface of the old desk. To him, this space was sacred. A myth, made real.

Geoffrey watched him, curious, unsure. The presence of this young man didn't feel like a disruption. It felt like a key. One that had been missing all along.

"You said you came through my teachings," Geoffrey finally asked. "From where? When?"

Cassian turned to him and smiled, his voice calm, his presence steady.

"I was born in 2139. The world is different now, fractured, but healing. We've come to understand that time isn't what we thought it was. And that healing doesn't move in one direction."

He stepped closer to the Book. Not the glowing, living version Geoffrey had seen in trance, but the worn, leather-bound one in his hands.

Cassian reached into his coat pocket and pulled out a small, crystalline object, shimmering faintly with light that didn't belong to this century.

"This is why I'm here." Cassian placed the crystal on the table. Immediately, the Book pulsed. The air thickened. Time slowed.

And then, something impossible happened: a new page appeared, one Geoffrey had never seen, one he hadn't written. On it was a title: "The Spectacles of Memory: The Guardian's Passage"

Geoffrey reached toward it, but his hand shook. "That chapter. It's from the future."

Cassian nodded. "You wrote it fifty years from now. It was sealed with intention, meant only to be opened at the moment you would understand it. That moment is now."

Cassian explained that The Loveday Method, as powerful as it already was, was never meant to be the end. It was the activation point, a way to remember the past, so the future could be shaped deliberately.

Not just to heal what had been, but to consciously plant what could be.

"The Method created a generation of returners," Cassian said. "People who learned to walk time like memory, to change timelines through healing, to prevent suffering before it could take root."

"But none of it could exist without you. Without this moment. Without your return to yourself."

He paused. "You weren't just meant to remember the past, Geoffrey. You were meant to teach us how to remember the future."

"But why now?" Geoffrey asked. "Why are you here? Why this moment?"

Cassian's expression turned solemn.

"Because there's a fracture forming. Something old is waking again, something that was never healed properly. It's echoing forward, pulling apart everything we've built. You are the only one who can reach that memory. Because it's yours. But you buried it lifetimes ago. We need you to go back one final time and bring forward the truth that was never spoken. The one that created the first silence."

Geoffrey felt the weight of the words. Not fear. Not pressure. Just a strange kind of gravity. Like a star collapsing inward. A soul returning home.

He looked at the crystal. Then at the Book. Then at the young man who knew his name before he ever spoke it.

"What happens if I find it?" Geoffrey asked.

Cassian smiled. "Then the world remembers. And time begins to heal itself."

Chapter Twenty Four: The First Silence

Before the Book was written, before the Method had a name, before any seeker walked the bridge between lives, there was one soul, one vow, and one forgotten wound that set it all in motion.

Geoffrey had guided hundreds, perhaps thousands, through time. But this was different.

This wasn't a soul memory rising to meet him. This wasn't someone else's pain calling for release.

This was a summons. One he had delayed for lifetimes. One that only now, with Cassian watching, the Book open and the crystal humming at his side, he could finally answer.

He sat down. Breathed in. Closed his eyes. And whispered to the soul: "Take me back. Back to the first wound. Back to where the silence began."

There was no staircase this time. No gentle descent. No guiding voice.

There was only light. Blinding. Soft. And full of knowing.

When the light faded, Geoffrey stood barefoot on cracked white stone. Beneath him: an endless desert.

Above: stars that shimmered like they were watching him.

In his hands: a pen made of fire. And around his neck, the spectacles.

He was not Geoffrey. He was not Alarion. Not yet. His name was Kael. And he was the first.

Kael belonged to an ancient civilisation long since erased from the surface of the earth, a culture that lived not by law, but by resonance. By soul-encoded memory.

They were scribes of truth. They didn't write history. They remembered it, before it happened.

And Kael was the youngest scribe ever chosen. Not because he had knowledge, but because he could hear the soul of time.

Every word he wrote carried power. Every truth he spoke shaped reality. But then he made one choice.

One terrible, human, loving choice. He kept something secret.

A truth he was meant to share. A message from the future. A glimpse of destruction.

But to speak it would have meant exile. So he held it. Buried it.

And that silence, that single withheld truth, was the first fracture.

The one that echoed down lifetimes.

Geoffrey, remembering as Kael, fell to his knees in the memory. The fire-pen slipped from his hand.

"I was afraid," he whispered. "I didn't want to lose them. So I stayed quiet. And the world changed."

Cassian's voice reached through the trance. "What was the truth, Kael?"

"That the timekeepers had lied. That the cycle of peace was ending. That we needed to awaken the others."

"But I said nothing. I choose comfort over calling. And I watched it all fall."

It was in the ashes of that fall, after the temples had crumbled, after the great knowledge had been scattered, that Kael made a vow:

"In every life that follows, I will guide others to remember. I will build the bridge I once refused to walk. And I will never silence the soul again."

That vow became a current. A pulse through every incarnation. Through Alarion. Through Geoffrey. Through every seeker who had walked into the Book.

And with it, The Loveday Method was born. Not in practice, but in purpose.

Geoffrey gasped as he emerged from trance. His hands trembled. Tears streamed silently down his face.

Cassian was waiting. Not with questions, but with stillness.

Geoffrey didn't speak for a long time. When he did, his voice was raw.

"I remember now. The silence wasn't theirs. It was mine. And I've been breaking it ever since."

The Book shimmered. A final page appeared, blank. Geoffrey reached for the crystal pen Cassian had brought from the future. It fit in his hand like it had been waiting all this time.

He wrote: "The soul remembers what the mind forgets. And when truth is finally spoken, time begins to heal.

This was the beginning. And this is the return. The Book is open. The silence has ended.

Chapter Twenty Five: The Echo in Your Hands

Some books don't just tell stories. They remember you.

So here we are, at the final page. Not an ending. A beginning.

You've walked through memory. You've seen lives unfold that were not yours, but somehow, you felt them anyway.

Perhaps that's because they were yours. Or echoes of them. Fragments left in your bones, in your dreams, in your breath.

This is more than a book. It always has been.

It is a remembering.

The Book of Echoes

Some say it's a myth. A book not written in ink, but woven into the fabric of time itself.

But you've held it. Page by page. Memory by memory.

The Book of Echoes is real, not because it exists in the world, but because it stirs in your soul.

Every time you breathe more freely, cry without knowing why, or feel seen by a story that shouldn't know you, the Book is open.

The Enchanted Spectacles

And what of the Spectacles? The ones whispered of in dreams, the lenses through which truth is finally clear?

They are not worn on the face. They are worn by the soul. They allow you to see the world not as it is, but as it truly has been. As it still could be.

You may already be wearing them. You wouldn't know it. Not at first.

But when the unseen becomes familiar, when the impossible feels intimate, you'll know.

The Coat of a Thousand Lives

And the coat? The one that appeared without warning, carried across lifetimes, worn by the brave and the broken and the ones who dared to remember?

That coat is no ordinary garment. It is a mark of remembrance. A soul-cloak. A quiet symbol that you are part of something much older and much more powerful than your current name.

You may not see it yet. But you've felt it. The shiver. The knowing. The sense that something ancient is draped across your shoulders, even when you walk alone.

That coat chooses those ready to walk between lifetimes. To heal. To remember. To lead others back.

If you've heard it calling, you're not imagining it. You're being called.

When The Loveday Method came to me, I thought I was the teacher. But I was the student. The translator. The keeper of a vow made long before this lifetime began.

Now, I pass this to you.

Not as knowledge, but as a thread. You are part of this story now. In fact, you always were.

I'm not asking you to believe. Only to remember.

And to wonder: What if this feeling in your chest is not fear, but memory? What if the grief that never made sense is inherited? What if the longing you carry isn't for a place, but for a time you've already lived?

You are not broken. You are not late. You are not alone.

You are remembering.

And your remembering will help others do the same.

So I'll leave you with this: You are the echo. You are the bridge. You are the next author of the Book.

When you're ready, close these pages.

But know this; the Book of Echoes, the Enchanted Spectacles, and the Coat of a Thousand Lives will never close on you.

Not now. Not ever.

Final Reflection

"The Thread Has Always Known Your Name"

You have walked through echoes. You have worn the Coat. Peered through the Spectacles. Opened the Book. And somewhere along the way, you may have felt it; a shiver, a stillness, a recognition.

Not just of the stories. But of yourself.

Because this journey was never only about the past. It was never only about other people's pain. It was about the part of you that has been waiting to awaken.

The part that remembers.

The grief that didn't start in this life. The fear you were told was "just anxiety." The dream that made no sense, until now.

The Loveday Method, at its heart, is not a technique.

It is a remembering.

It is the moment you step through the veil and realise the answers were never lost, only sleeping in the deeper chambers of your soul.

It is the bridge between lifetimes. Between the breath of the body and the memory of the eternal.

And now, you stand at that bridge. Not to look back, but to walk forward, knowing more of who you truly are.

So what now?

Perhaps you follow the thread. Perhaps you sit in stillness and listen for the voice beneath your thoughts. Perhaps you guide others, just as you have been guided.

Because the world is full of those still carrying stories that were never theirs. Still searching for a reason behind the ache they can't explain.

And now you know: It's not madness. It's memory. And memory can be healed. Not through forgetting, but through the sacred act of remembering and returning it to time.

So, whether this book was your beginning or only a return to something you've always known, may you walk forward with open eyes? May you listen to what speaks without words? May you trust the ache is not the end, but the invitation?

And above all, may you know this: You were never lost. You were only waiting for the thread to call you home.

— Geoffrey Loveday

Dedication

To those who carry silent stories; may you one day find the words to speak them.

To the ones haunted by dreams not their own, you are not broken. You are remembering.

And to the forgotten: You were never truly lost.

This is for you.

About the Author

Geoffrey E. Loveday has spent much of his life listening – to people, to silence, and to the quiet language of the unseen.

His work began not as a profession but as a personal search for understanding – a way to make sense of the patterns of sorrow, love, and longing that seem to pass from one generation to the next.

Through years of experience, study, and deep reflection, that search grew into what is now known as The Loveday Method – a process that helps others explore the hidden landscapes of memory, emotion, and ancestry.

Guiding people through these journeys, Geoffrey has watched them rediscover forgotten parts of themselves, reconnect with their lineage, and release the inherited pain that has quietly shaped their lives.

He writes from a simple but profound belief: that healing is the natural movement of life itself; that every story, no matter how distant, longs to be heard and set free.

His books are part story, part meditation, and part invitation – written for anyone who has ever sensed that there is more to life than what meets the eye.

Today, Geoffrey continues his work of helping others to remember who they are – to walk the bridge between past and present, between the visible and the unseen.

His message is constant and clear: that love is the true bridge between all worlds, and that every act of compassion, every moment of forgiveness, brings humanity one step closer to wholeness.

For further information about the Loveday Method, upcoming writings, or future events, contact at:

- www.liverpoolhypnosis.co.uk
- www.mindlayers.com
- thelovedaymethod.com
- inheritedtherapy.com
- Mobile: 07876028957

Coming In 2025

A Journey Beyond Time:

Healing the Past to Free the Present

Fiction or Real? You Decide.

The Origin of

The Loveday Method®

The Thirteenth Book

www.ingramcontent.com/pod-product-compliance
Lightning Source LLC
Chambersburg PA
CBHW041306240426
43661CB00011B/1033